CSET 120-124

Biology-Life Science
Teacher Certification Exam

By: Sharon Wynne, M.S.
Southern Connecticut State University

"And, while there's no reason yet to panic, I think it's only prudent that we make preparations to panic."

XAMonline, INC.
Boston

XAMonline, Inc.
21 Orient Ave.
Melrose, MA 02176
Toll Free 1-800-509-4128
Email: winwin1111@aol.com
Web www.xamonline.com
Fax: 1-718-662-9268

Library of Congress Cataloging-in-Publication Data

Wynne, Sharon A.
    Biology-Life Science 120-124: Teacher Certification / Sharon A. Wynne. -2nd ed.
    ISBN 978-1-58197-809-4
    1. Biology-Life Science 120-124.   2. Study Guides.   3. CSET
    4. Teachers' Certification & Licensure.   5. Careers

Disclaimer:
The material presented in this publication is the sole work of XAMonline and was created independently from the National Education Association, Educational Testing Service, or any State Department of Education, National Evaluation Systems or other testing affiliates.

Between the time of publication and printing, state specific standards, testing formats, and website information may change. XAMonline developed the sample test questions and they reflect similar content as on real tests; however, they are not former tests. XAMonline assembles content that aligns with state standards, but makes no claims nor guarantees regarding test performance. Numerical scores are determined by testing companies such as NES or ETS and then are compared with individual state standards. A passing score varies from state to state.

Printed in the United States of America

CSET: Biology-Life Science 120-124
ISBN: 978-1-58197-585-7

Table of Contents

DOMAIN II - Subject Matter Skills and Abilities

Tips for creating a great essay!

Essay writing is an important assessment tool in the educational realm. You have undoubtedly written many essays in your undergraduate career. California requires candidates to create essays as part of the teacher certification examination for its biology subtest 124. You will also need to know how to write a proper essay so you can evaluate and critique your students' essays. Here are some important aspects to consider.

What is the question? Make sure you answer the question fully. When you are brainstorming, it is easy to get off track. This is not necessarily a bad thing as it allows you to search your mind for all pertinent information. However, instructors do not want to read everything you know. They want you to answer the question they asked. Read the question before answering it, ponder, write, and then read the question AGAIN. Ask yourself if you have answered it.

Use strong writing skills and proper grammar. For those of you who have relied extensively on spell check, recognize that this may not always be available, and double-check your work. Writing needs to be clear to the reader. Ask yourself the following questions. Is it clear and concise? Does it flow well and have organization? You should reiterate the question as a statement in your first sentence, and then work your way through the essay in a way that makes sense, touching on all points.

Look for key words. There will be key words in the question that tell you how to proceed. For example, the essay question may begin with any of the following: compare, contrast, explain, identify, reconcile, define, describe, or hypothesize.

Compare: the assessor is looking for a comparison between two or more objects/ideas. How are they similar?

Contrast: the assessor is looking for a comparison between two or more items/ideas. How are they different?

Explain: the assessor is looking for a thorough definition of the term/process. It should be a summary.

Identify: the assessor is asking for you to suggest applicable answers. Make sure you read the question and understand what is applicable before you begin the identification.

Reconcile: the assessor is asking for you to examine how multiple pieces work together. Often the subjects seem in opposition but are both crucial. It is kind of like a jigsaw puzzle; there is a solution! Think both in and out of the box for this one!

Define: this requires a flat out definition. Nothing too elaborate, but enough to be precise. Being concise is the key; use as few words as possible to relay the information accurately.

Describe: a description is more elaborate than a definition. It requires more aesthetic information. For example, you would define a cat differently than you would describe one. Adjectives are appropriate.

Hypothesize: you are expected to make a prediction. It is based on accumulated knowledge, so you can really shine here! The key is to use solid data and a well thought-out, logical process. You can argue your hypothesis with evidence.

Good Luck!

Great Study and Testing Tips!

What to study in order to prepare for the subject assessments is the focus of this study guide, but equally important is *how* you study.

You can increase your chances of truly mastering the information by taking some simple, but effective steps.

Study Tips:

1. <u>Some foods aid the learning process</u>. Foods such as milk, nuts, seeds, rice, and oats help your study efforts by releasing natural memory enhancers called CCKs (*cholecystokinins*) composed of *tryptophan*, *choline*, and *phenylalanine*. All of these chemicals enhance the neurotransmitters associated with memory. Before studying, try a light, protein-rich meal of eggs, turkey, and fish. All of these foods release the memory enhancing chemicals. The better the connections, the more you comprehend.

Likewise, before you take a test, stick to a light snack of energy boosting and relaxing foods. A glass of milk, a piece of fruit, or some peanuts all release various memory-boosting chemicals and help you relax and focus on the subject at hand.

2. <u>Learn to take great notes</u>. A by-product of our modern culture is that we have grown accustomed to getting our information in short doses (e.g., TV news sound bites or USA Today style newspaper articles).

Consequently, we've subconsciously trained ourselves to assimilate information better in <u>neat little packages</u>. If your notes are scrawled all over the paper, it fragments the flow of the information. Strive for clarity. Newspapers use a standard format to achieve clarity. Your notes can be much clearer through use of proper formatting. A very effective format is called the *"Cornell Method."*

> Take a sheet of loose-leaf lined notebook paper and draw a line all the way down the paper about 1-2" from the left-hand edge.

> Draw another line across the width of the paper about 1-2" up from the bottom. Repeat this process on the reverse side of the page.

Look at the highly effective result. You have ample room for notes, a left hand margin for special emphasis items or inserting supplementary data from the textbook, a large area at the bottom for a brief summary, and a little rectangular space for just about anything you want.

3. <u>Get the concept, then the details</u>. Too often we focus on the details and fail to gather an understanding of the concept. If you simply memorize dates, places, and names, you may well miss the whole point of the subject.

Putting concepts in your own words can increase your understanding. If you are working from a textbook, automatically summarize each paragraph in your mind. If you are outlining text, don't simply copy the author's words, *rephrase* them in your own words.

You remember your own thoughts and words much better than someone else's, and subconsciously tend to associate the important details to the core concepts.

4. <u>Ask Why?</u> Pull apart written material paragraph by paragraph and don't forget the captions under the illustrations.

Example: If the heading is "Stream Erosion", flip it around to read "Why do streams erode?" Then answer the question.

If you train your mind to think in a series of questions and answers, not only will you learn more, but you will decrease your test anxiety by increasing your familiarity with the question and answer process.

5. <u>Read for reinforcement and future needs</u>. Even if you only have ten minutes, put your notes or a book in your hand. Your mind is similar to a computer, you have to input data in order to process it. *By reading, you are creating the neural connections for future retrieval.* The more times you read something, the more you reinforce the learning of ideas.

Even if you don't fully understand something on the first pass, *your mind stores much of the material for later recall.*

6. <u>Relax and go into exile to learn</u>. Our bodies respond to an inner clock called biorhythms. Burning the midnight oil works well for some people, but not everyone.

If possible, set aside a particular place to study that is free of distractions. Shut off the television, cell phone, and pager and exile your friends and family during your study period.

If silence really bothers you, try background music. Light classical music at a low volume has been shown to aid in concentration. Music that evokes pleasant emotions without lyrics is highly suggested. Try just about anything by Mozart. It relaxes you.

7. <u>**Use arrows, not highlighters.**</u> At best, it's difficult to read a page full of yellow, pink, blue, and green streaks. Try staring at a neon sign for a while and you'll soon see that the horde of colors obscure the message.

A quick note, a brief dash of color, an underline, and an arrow pointing to a particular passage is much clearer than a horde of highlighted words.

8. <u>**Budget your study time.**</u> Although you shouldn't ignore any of the material, *allocate your available study time in the same ratio that topics may appear on the test.*

Testing Tips:

1. <u>Get smart, play dumb</u>. Don't read anything into the question. Don't make an assumption that the test writer is looking for something else than what is asked.

2. <u>Read the question and all the choices *twice* before answering the question</u>. You may miss something by not carefully reading and re-reading both the question and the answers.

If you really don't have a clue as to the right answer, leave it blank on the first time through. Go on to the other questions, as they may provide a clue as to how to answer the skipped questions.

If later on, you still can't answer the skipped ones . . . *Guess.* The only penalty for guessing is that you *might* get it wrong. Only one thing is certain; if you don't put anything down, you will get it wrong!

3. <u>Turn the question into a statement</u>. Look at the wording of the questions. The syntax of the question usually provides a clue. Does it seem more familiar as a statement rather than as a question? Does it sound strange?

By turning a question into a statement, you may be able to spot if an answer sounds right, and it may also trigger memories of material you have read.

4. <u>Look for hidden clues</u>. It's actually very difficult to compose multiple-foil (choice) questions without giving away part of the answer in the options presented.

In most multiple-choice questions you can often readily eliminate one or two of the potential answers. This leaves you with only two real possibilities and automatically your odds go to fifty-fifty with very little work.

5. <u>Trust your instincts</u>. On questions that you aren't really certain about, go with your basic instincts. **Your first impression on how to answer a question is usually correct.**

6. <u>Mark your answers directly on the test booklet</u>. Don't bother trying to fill in the optical scan sheet on the first pass through the test.

Just be very careful not to miss-mark your answers when you eventually transcribe them to the scan sheet.

7. <u>Watch the clock</u>! You have a set amount of time to answer the questions. Don't get bogged down trying to answer a single question at the expense of 10 questions you can more readily answer.

DOMAIN I –Subject Matter Understanding and Skill in Biology/Life Science

Competency 1.0   Cell Biology and Physiology

Skill 1.1   Prokaryotic and Eukaryotic Cells

a. Compare prokaryotic cells, eukaryotic cells, and viruses in terms of complexity, general structure, differentiation, and their requirements for growth and replication

The cell is the basic unit of all living things. There are three types of cells: prokaryotic, eukaryotic, and archaea. Archaea have some similarities with prokaryotes, but are as distantly related to prokaryotes as prokaryotes are to eukaryotes.

PROKARYOTES

Prokaryotes consist only of bacteria and cyanobacteria (formerly known as blue-green algae). The diagram below shows the classification of prokaryotes.

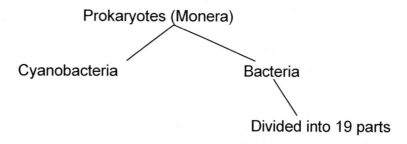

Bacterial cells have no defined nucleus or nuclear membrane. The DNA, RNA, and ribosomes float freely within the cell. The cytoplasm has a single chromosome condensed to form a **nucleoid**. Prokaryotes have a thick cell wall made up of amino sugars (glycoproteins) that provides protection, gives the cell shape, and keeps the cell from bursting. An application of this is the use of the antibiotic penicillin to target the **cell wall** of bacteria, disrupting the cell wall, and thereby killing the cell.

The cell wall surrounds the **cell membrane** (plasma membrane). The cell membrane consists of a lipid bilayer that controls the passage of molecules in and out of the cell. Some prokaryotes have a capsule made of polysaccharides that surrounds the cell wall for extra protection from higher organisms.

Many bacterial cells have appendages used for movement called **flagella**. Some cells also have **pili**, which are a protein strand used for attachment. Pili may also be used for sexual conjugation (where bacterial cells exchange DNA). Prokaryotes are the most numerous and widespread organisms on earth. Bacteria were most likely the first cells and date back in the fossil record to 3.5 billion years ago. Their ability to adapt to the environment allows them to thrive in a wide variety of habitats.

Most bacteria absorb nutrients from the environment through small channels in their cell walls and membranes (chemotrophs) while some perform photosynthesis (phototrophs). Chemoorganotrophs use organic compounds as energy sources while chemolithotrophs can use inorganic chemicals as energy sources. Depending on the type of metabolism and energy source, bacteria release a variety of waste products (e.g. alcohols, acids, carbon dioxide) to the environment through diffusion.

All bacteria reproduce through binary fission (asexual reproduction) producing two identical cells. Bacteria reproduce very rapidly, dividing or doubling every twenty minutes in optimal conditions. Asexual reproduction does not allow for genetic variation, but bacteria achieve genetic variety by absorbing DNA from ruptured cells and conjugating or swapping chromosomal or plasmid DNA with other cells.

EUKARYOTES

Eukaryotic cells are found in protists, fungi, plants, and animals. Most eukaryotic cells are larger than prokaryotic cells. They contain many organelles, which are membrane-bound areas for specific functions. Their cytoplasm contains a cytoskeleton which provides a protein framework for the cell. The cytoplasm also supports the organelles and contains the ions and molecules necessary for cell function. The cytoplasm is contained by the plasma membrane. The plasma membrane allows molecules to pass in and out of the cell. The membrane can bud inward to engulf outside material in a process called endocytosis. Exocytosis is a secretory mechanism, the reverse of endocytosis.

The most significant differentiation between prokaryotes and eukaryotes is that eukaryotes have a **nucleus**. The nucleus is the "brain" of the cell that contains all of the cell's genetic information. Inside the nucleus are the chromosomes which consist of chromatin, complexes of DNA and proteins. The chromosomes are tightly coiled to conserve space while providing a large surface area. The nucleus is the site of transcription of the DNA into RNA. The **nucleolus** found inside the nucleus is where ribosomes are made. There is at least one of these dark-staining bodies inside the nucleus of most eukaryotes. The nuclear envelope around the nucleus consists of two membranes separated by a narrow space. The envelope contains many pores that let RNA out of the nucleus.

Ribosomes are the site for protein synthesis. Ribosomes may be free-floating in the cytoplasm or attached to the endoplasmic reticulum. There may be as many as a half a million ribosomes in a cell, depending on how much protein the cell makes.

The **endoplasmic reticulum** (ER) is folded and has a large surface area. It is the "roadway" of the cell and allows for transport of materials through and out of the cell. There are two types of ER: smooth and rough. Smooth endoplasmic reticula contain no ribosomes on their surface and are the site of lipid synthesis. Rough endoplasmic reticula have ribosomes on their surface and aid in the synthesis of proteins that are membrane-bound or destined for secretion.

Many of the products made in the ER proceed to the Golgi apparatus. The **Golgi apparatus** functions to sort, modify, and package molecules that are made in the other parts of the cell (like the ER). These molecules are either sent out of the cell or to other organelles within the cell.

Lysosomes are found mainly in animal cells. These contain digestive enzymes that break down food, unnecessary substances, viruses, damaged cell components, and, eventually, the cell itself. It is believed that lysosomes play a role in the aging process.

Mitochondria are large organelles that are the site of cellular respiration, the production of ATP that supplies energy to the cell. Muscle cells have many mitochondria because they use a great deal of energy. Mitochondria have their own DNA, RNA, and ribosomes and are capable of reproducing by binary fission if there is a great demand for additional energy. Mitochondria have two membranes: a smooth outer membrane and a folded inner membrane. The folds inside the mitochondria are called cristae. They provide a large surface area for cellular respiration to occur.

Plastids are found only in photosynthetic organisms such as plants. They are similar to the mitochondira due to the double membrane structure. They also have their own DNA, RNA, and ribosomes and can reproduce if the need for the increased capture of sunlight becomes necessary. There are several types of plastids. **Chloroplasts** are the site of photosynthesis. The stroma is the chloroplast's inner membrane space. The stoma encloses sacs called thylakoids that contain the photosynthetic pigment chlorophyll. The chlorophyll traps sunlight inside the thylakoid to generate ATP which is used in the stroma to produce carbohydrates and other products. The **chromoplasts** make and store yellow and orange pigments. They provide color to leaves, flowers, and fruits. The **amyloplasts** store starch and are used as a food reserve. They are abundant in roots like potatoes.

The Endosymbiotic Theory states that mitochondria and chloroplasts were once free living and possibly evolved from prokaryotic cells. At some point in evolutionary history, they entered the eukaryotic cell and maintained a symbiotic relationship with the cell, with both the cell and organelle benefiting from the relationship. The fact that they both have their own DNA, RNA, ribosomes, and are capable of reproduction supports this theory.

Found only in plant cells, the **cell wall** is composed of cellulose and fibers. It is thick enough for support and protection, yet porous enough to allow water and dissolved substances to enter. **Vacuoles** are found mostly in plant cells. They hold stored food and pigments. Their large size allows them to fill with water in order to provide turgor pressure. Lack of turgor pressure causes a plant to wilt.

The **cytoskeleton**, found in both animal and plant cells, is composed of protein filaments attached to the plasma membrane and organelles. The cytoskeleton provides a framework for the cell and aids in cell movement. Three types of fibers make up the cytoskeleton:

1. **Microtubules** – The largest of the three fibers, they make up cilia and flagella for locomotion. Some examples are sperm cells, cilia that line the fallopian tubes, and tracheal cilia. Centrioles are also composed of microtubules. They aid in cell division to form the spindle fibers that pull the cell apart into two new cells. Centrioles are not found in the cells of higher plants.

2. **Intermediate filaments** – Intermediate in size, they are smaller than microtubules, but larger than microfilaments. They help the cell keep its shape.

3. **Microfilaments** – Smallest of the three fibers, they are made of actin and small amounts of myosin (like in muscle tissue). They function in cell movement like cytoplasmic streaming, endocytosis, and ameboid movement. This structure pinches the two cells apart after cell division, forming two new cells.

The following is a diagram of a generalized animal cell.

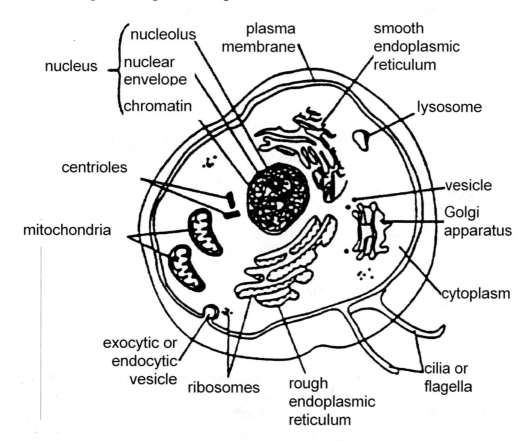

Animals are multicellular, eukaryotic organisms. All animals obtain nutrients by eating food (ingestion). Different types of animals derive nutrients from eating plants, other animals, or both. Animal cells perform respiration that converts food molecules, mainly carbohydrates and fats, into energy. The excretory systems of animals, like animals themselves, vary in complexity. Simple invertebrates eliminate waste through a single tube, while complex vertebrates have a specialized system of organs that process and excrete waste.

Most animals, unlike bacteria, exist in two distinct sexes. Members of the female sex give birth or lay eggs. Some less developed animals can reproduce asexually. For example, flatworms can divide in two and some unfertilized insect eggs can develop into viable organisms. Most animals reproduce sexually through various mechanisms. For example, aquatic animals reproduce by external fertilization of eggs, while mammals reproduce by internal fertilization. More developed animals possess specialized reproductive systems and cycles that facilitates reproduction and promotes genetic variation.

Plants, like animals, are multi-cellular, eukaryotic organisms. Plants obtain nutrients from the soil through their root systems and convert sunlight into energy through photosynthesis. Many plants store waste products in vacuoles or organs (e.g. leaves, bark) that are discarded. Some plants also excrete waste through their roots.

More than half of the plant species reproduce by producing seeds from which new plants grow. Depending on the type of plant, flowers or cones produce seeds. Other plants reproduce by spores, tubers, bulbs, buds, and grafts. The flowers of flowering plants contain the reproductive organs. Pollination is the joining of male and female gametes that is often facilitated by movement by wind or animals.

Fungi are eukaryotic, mostly multi-cellular organisms. All fungi are heterotrophs, obtaining nutrients from other organisms. More specifically, most fungi obtain nutrients by digesting and absorbing nutrients from dead organisms. Fungi secrete enzymes outside of their body to digest organic material and then absorb the nutrients through their cell walls.

Most fungi can reproduce asexually and sexually. Different types of fungi reproduce asexually by mitosis, budding, sporification, or fragmentation. Sexual reproduction of fungi is different from sexual reproduction of animals. The two mating types of fungi are plus and minus, not male and female. The fusion of hyphae, the specialized reproductive structure in fungi, between plus and minus types produces and scatters diverse spores.

Protists are eukaryotic, single-celled organisms. Most protists are heterotrophic, obtaining nutrients by ingesting small molecules and cells and digesting them in vacuoles. All protists reproduce asexually by either binary or multiple fission. Like bacteria, protists achieve genetic variation by exchange of DNA through conjugation.

ARCHAEA

There are three kinds of organisms with archaea cells: **methanogens**, obligate anaerobes that produce methane, **halobacteria**, which can live only in concentrated brine solutions, and **thermoacidophiles**, which can live only in acidic hot springs.

VIRUSES

Microbiology includes the study of monera, protists, and viruses. Although **viruses** are not classified as living things, they greatly affect other living things by disrupting cell activity. Viruses are obligate parasites because they rely on the host for their own reproduction. Viruses are composed of a protein coat and a nucleic acid, either DNA or RNA. A bacteriophage is a virus that infects a bacterium. Animal viruses are classified by the type of nucleic acid, presence of RNA replicase, and presence of a protein coat.

There are two types of viral reproductive cycles:

1.   **Lytic cycle** - The virus enters the host cell and makes copies of its nucleic acids and protein coats and reassembles them into copies of itself. It then lyses or breaks out of the host cell and infects other nearby cells, repeating the process.

2.   **Lysogenic cycle** - The virus may remain dormant within the cell (often for months or years) until some factor activates it and stimulates it to break out of the cell. Herpes is an example of a lysogenic virus.

Skill 1.2   Cellular Reproduction

a. Describe the stages of the cell cycle

The purposes of cell division are to provide growth and repair in body (somatic) cells and to replenish or create sex cells for reproduction. There are two forms of cell division: mitosis and meiosis. **Mitosis** is the division of somatic cells and **meiosis** is the division of sex cells (eggs and sperm).

b. Diagram and describe the stages of the mitotic process

Mitosis is divided into two parts: the **mitotic (M) phase** and **interphase**. In the mitotic phase, mitosis and cytokinesis divide the nucleus and cytoplasm, respectively. This phase is the shortest phase of the cell cycle. Interphase is the stage where the cell grows and copies the chromosomes in preparation for the mitotic phase. Interphase occurs in three stages of growth: the **G1** (growth) period, when the cell grows and metabolizes, the **S** (synthesis) period, when the cell makes new DNA, and the **G2** (growth) period, when the cell makes new proteins and organelles in preparation for cell division.

The mitotic phase is a continuum of change, although we divide it into five distinct stages: prophase, prometaphase, metaphase, anaphase, and telophase.

During **prophase**, the cell proceeds through the following steps continuously, without stopping. First, the chromatin condenses to become visible chromosomes. Next, the nucleolus disappears and the nuclear membrane breaks apart. Then, mitotic spindles composed of microtubules form that will eventually pull the chromosomes apart. Finally, the cytoskeleton breaks down and the action of centrioles pushes the spindles to the poles or opposite ends of the cell.

During **prometaphase**, the nuclear membrane fragments and allows the spindle microtubules to interact with the chromosomes. Kinetochore fibers attach to the chromosomes at the centromere region. **Metaphase** begins when the centrosomes are at opposite ends of the cell. The centromeres of all the chromosomes are aligned with one another.

During **anaphase**, the centromeres split in half and homologous chromosomes separate. The chromosomes are pulled to the poles of the cell, with identical sets at either end. The last stage of mitosis is **telophase**. Here, two nuclei form with a full set of DNA that is identical to the parent cell. The nucleoli become visible and the nuclear membrane reassembles. A cell plate is seen in plant cells and a cleavage furrow forms in animal cells. The cell pinches into two cells. Finally, cytokinesis, or division of the cytoplasm and organelles, occurs.

Below is a diagram of mitosis.

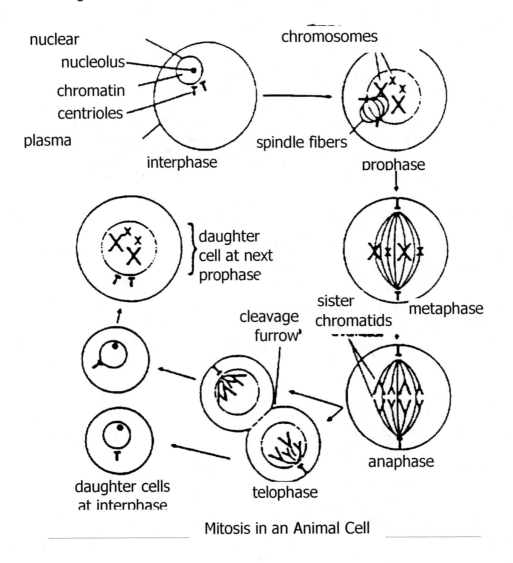

Mitosis in an Animal Cell

Meiosis is similar to mitosis, but there are two consecutive cell divisions, meiosis I and meiosis II in order to reduce the chromosome number by one half. This way, when the haploid sperm and haploid egg join during fertilization, so the diploid number is reached.

Similar to mitosis, meiosis is preceded by an interphase during which the chromosome replicates. The steps of meiosis are as follows:

1. **Prophase I** – The replicated chromosomes condense and pair with homologues in a process called synapsis. This forms a tetrad. Crossing over, the exchange of genetic material between homologues to further increase diversity, occurs during prophase I if it is going to occur.
2. **Metaphase I** – The homologous pairs attach to spindle fibers after lining up in the middle of the cell.
3. **Anaphase I** – The sister chromatids remain joined and move to the poles of the cell.
4. **Telophase I** – The homologous chromosome pairs continue to separate. Each pole now has a haploid chromosome set. Telophase I occurs simultaneously with cytokinesis. In animal cells, a cleavage furrow forms and, in plant cells, a cell plate appears.
5. **Prophase II** – A spindle apparatus forms and the chromosomes condense.
6. **Metaphase II** – Sister chromatids line up in center of cell. The centromeres divide and the sister chromatids begin to separate.
7. **Anaphase II** – The separated chromosomes move to opposite ends of the cell.
8. **Telophase II** – Cytokinesis occurs, resulting in four haploid daughter cells.

Below is a diagram of meiosis.

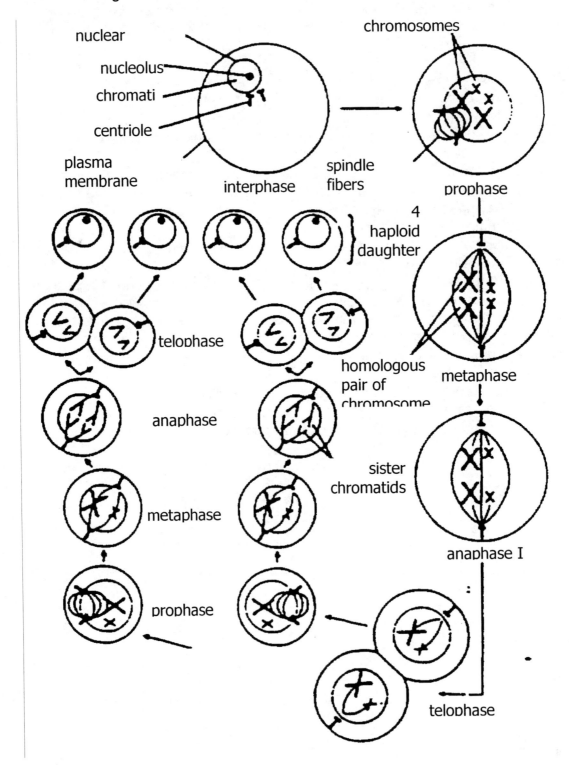

Skill 1.3   Plant and Animal Cell Anatomy and Physiology

a. Diagram the structure of the cell membrane and relate the structure to its function

In order to understand cellular transport, it is important to know about the structure of the cell membrane. All organisms contain cell membranes because they regulate the flow of materials into and out of the cell. The current model for the cell membrane is the Fluid Mosaic Model, which takes into account the ability of lipids and proteins to move and change places, giving the membrane fluidity.

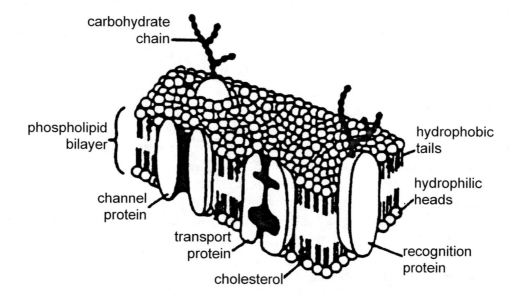

Cell membranes have the following characteristics:

1. They are made of phospholipids which have polar, ionically charged heads with a phosphate group which is hydrophilic (water loving) and two nonpolar lipid tails which are hydrophobic (water fearing). This allows the membrane to orient itself with the polar heads facing the fluid inside and outside the cell and the hydrophobic lipid tails sandwiched in between. Hydrogen bonding holds the membrane together. Each individual phospholipid is called a micelle.

2. They contain proteins embedded inside (integral proteins) and proteins on the surface (peripheral proteins). These proteins may act as channels for transport, may contain enzymes, may act as receptor sites, may act to stick cells together, or may attach to the cytoskeleton to give the cell shape.

3. They contain cholesterol, which alters the fluidity of the membrane.

4. They contain oligosaccharides (small carbohydrate polymers) on the outside of the membrane. These act as markers that help distinguish one cell from another.

5. They contain receptors made of glycoproteins that can attach to certain molecules, like hormones.

b. Explain methods of transport across the membrane (e.g., diffusion, active transport, endocytosis and exocytosis)

Cell transport is necessary to maintain homeostasis, or balance between the cell and its external environment. Cell membranes are selectively permeable, which is the key to transport. Not all molecules may pass through easily. Some molecules require energy or carrier molecules and may only cross when needed.

Passive transport does not require energy and moves the material with the concentration gradient (high to low). Small molecules may pass through the membrane in this manner. Two examples of passive transport include diffusion and osmosis. **Diffusion** is the ability of molecules to move from areas of high concentration to areas of low concentration. It normally involves small uncharged particles like oxygen. **Osmosis** is simply the diffusion of water across a semi-permeable membrane. Osmosis may cause cells to swell or shrink, depending on the internal and external environments. The following terms are used to describe the relationship of the cell to the environment.

Isotonic - Water concentration is equal inside and outside the cell. Net movement in either direction is basically equal.

Hypertonic - "Hyper" refers to the amount of dissolved particles. The more particles in a solution, the lower its water concentration. Therefore, when a cell is hypertonic to its environment, there is more water outside the cell than inside. Water will move into the cell and the cell will swell. If the environment is hypertonic to the cell, there is more water inside the cell. Water will move out of the cell and the cell will shrink.

Hypotonic - "Hypo" again refers to the amount of dissolved particles. The fewer particles there are in a solution, the higher its water concentration. When a cell is hypotonic to its environment, there is more water inside the cell than outside. Water will move out of the cell and the cell will shrink. If the environment is hypotonic to the cell, there is more water outside the cell than inside. Water will move into the cell and the cell will swell.

The **facilitated diffusion** mechanism does not require energy, but does require a carrier protein. An example is insulin, which is needed to carry glucose into the cell.

Active transport requires energy. The energy for this process comes from either ATP or an electrical charge difference. Active transport may move materials either with or against a concentration gradient. Some examples of active transport are:

- Sodium-Potassium pump - maintains an electrical difference across the cell. This is useful in restoring ion balance so nerves can continue to function. It exchanges sodium ions for potassium ions across the plasma membrane in animal cells.

- Stomach acid pump - exports hydrogen ions to lower the pH of the stomach and increase acidity.

- Calcium pumps - actively pump calcium outside of the cell and are important in nerve and muscle transmission.

Active transport involves a membrane potential, which is a charge on the membrane. The charge works like a magnet and may cause transport proteins to alter their shape, thus allowing substances into or out of the cell.

The transport of large molecules depends on the fluidity of the membrane, which is controlled by cholesterol in the membrane. **Exocytosis** is the release of large particles by vesicles fusing with the plasma membrane. In the process of **endocytosis**, the cell takes in macromolecules and particulate matter by forming vesicles derived from the plasma membrane. There are three types of endocytosis in animal cells. **Phagocytosis** is when a particle is engulfed by pseudopodia and packaged in a vacuole. In **pinocytosis**, the cell takes in extracellular fluid in small vesicles. **Receptor-mediated endocytosis** is when the membrane vesicles bud inward to allow a cell to take in large amounts of certain substances. The vesicles have proteins with receptors that are specific for the substance.

c. Explain the role of semipermeable membranes in cellular communication

Cellular communication is the interaction of cells facilitated by the release, diffusion, and reception of molecules. The semipermeable nature of cell membranes is an important aspect of the regulation of cellular communication. Semipermeability means that only some types of molecules can cross the membrane barrier and enter the cell. Because most signal molecules are large and water-soluble, they cannot readily cross semipermeable membranes. This selectiveness allows cells to identify and distinguish between the myriad signal molecules present in the cellular environment.

Because not all molecules can cross semipermeable cell membranes, only the molecules designed to signal a particular cell have the ability to communicate. Cell membranes possess surface receptors that recognize certain molecules.

Cell membrane surface receptors recognize and bind local regulator proteins or systemic hormones and transfer the "message" to the cell that in turn generates a response. Binding of signal molecules may directly induce cellular activity or open protein channels in the membrane allowing the entrance of certain molecules.

d. Explain the role of the endoplasmic reticulum and Golgi apparatus in the secretion of proteins

Two of the most important locations within a eukaryotic cell are the endoplasmic reticulum and Golgi apparatus. The **endoplasmic reticulum** (ER) is folded a great number of times, but the membrane forms a single sheet which encloses a single sac, thereby giving the sac a large surface area. It is the "roadway" of the cell and allows for transport of materials through and out of the cell. There are two types of ER: smooth and rough. Smooth endoplasmic reticula contain no ribosomes on their surface and are the site of lipid synthesis. Rough endoplasmic reticula have ribosomes on their surface and aid in the synthesis of proteins that are membrane-bound or destined for secretion. The products made in the ER proceed to the Golgi apparatus, the plasma membrane, the lysosomes, or wherever they are needed.

The **Golgi apparatus** functions to sort, modify, and package molecules that are made in the other parts of the cell (like the ER). These molecules are either sent out of the cell or to other organelles within the cell. The Golgi apparatus is actually a complex of numerous sets of smooth disc-shaped cisternae which are coated with lipid membranes. It also contains a great many vesicles which are used to send molecules to the cellular membrane to be excreted. The Golgi apparatus functions to direct molecules into and throughout the cell. Various molecules are "sorted" by vesicles which each have specific receptors that attach to specific molecules in order to move them where they are needed.

e. Explain the role of chloroplasts in obtaining and storing usable energy

In photosynthetic organisms, **chloroplasts** are the site of photosynthesis. The stroma is the space between the chloroplast's inner membrane and the chloroplast's permeable outer membrane. The stoma encloses sacs called thylakoids that contain the photosynthetic pigment chlorophyll. The chlorophyll traps sunlight inside the thylakoid, a membrane that forms a series of flattened discs, to generate ATP (adenotriphosphate) which is used in the stroma to produce carbohydrates and other products. The **chromoplasts** make and store yellow and orange pigments. They provide color to leaves, flowers, and fruits. The **amyloplasts** store starch and are used as a food reserve. They are abundant in roots like potatoes.

f. Explain the role of mitochondria in cellular respiration

Mitochondria are large organelles that are the site of cellular respiration, the production of ATP that supplies energy to the cell. Muscle cells have many mitochondria because they use a great deal of energy. Mitochondria have their own DNA, RNA, and ribosomes and are capable of reproducing by binary fission if there is a great demand for additional energy. Mitochondria have two membranes: a smooth outer membrane and a folded inner membrane. The outer membrane contains many large transport proteins to allow for large molecules to enter. It also includes proteins for converting lipid substrates into forms to be used by the matrix. The folds inside the mitochondrial inner membrane are called cristae. They provide a large surface area for cellular respiration to occur. Oxidation phosphorylation takes place here. Three major proteins are found here: (1) the proteins involved in the oxidation reactions of the respiratory chain, (2) the enzyme complex ATP synthetase for making ATP, and (3) the transport proteins for regulating the transfer into and out of the matrix. The matrix is the site of the Kreb Cycle and it contains copies of the mitochondrial DNA genome, specialized ribosomes, tRNAs, and various enzymes.

g. Explain the role of enzymes in chemical reactions and describe an experiment to test the catalytic role of enzymes and factors that affect enzyme activity (e.g., levels of protein organization, temperature, ionic conditions, concentration of enzyme and substrate, pH)

Enzymes act as biological catalysts to speed up reactions. Enzymes are the most diverse of all types of proteins. They are not used up in a reaction and are recyclable. Each enzyme is specific for a single reaction. Enzymes act on a substrate. The substrate is the material to be broken down or put back together. Most enzymes end in the suffix -ase (lipase, amylase). The prefix is the substrate being acted on (lipids, sugars).

$$\text{Substrate} \xrightarrow{\text{Enzyme}} \text{Product}$$

The active site is the region of the enzyme that binds to the substrate. There are two theories for how the active site functions. The **lock and key theory** states that the shape of the enzyme is specific because it fits into the substrate like a key fits into a lock. It aids in holding molecules close together so reactions can easily occur. The **Induced fit theory** states that an enzyme can stretch and bend to fit the substrate. This is the most accepted theory.

Many factors can affect enzyme activity. Temperature and pH are two of those factors. The temperature can affect the rate of reaction of an enzyme. The optimal pH for enzymes is between 6 and 8, with only a few enzymes whose optimal pH falls out of this range.

Cofactors aid in the enzyme's function. Cofactors may be inorganic or organic. Organic cofactors are known as coenzymes. Vitamins are examples of coenzymes. Some chemicals can inhibit an enzyme's function. **Competitive inhibitors** block the substrate from entering the active site of the enzyme to reduce productivity. **Noncompetitive inhibitors** bind to the enzyme in a location not in the active site but still in a place that will interrupt substrate binding. In most cases, noncompetitive inhibitors alter the shape of the enzyme. An **allosteric enzyme** can exist in two shapes, one in which they are active and one in which they are inactive. Overactive enzymes may cause metabolic diseases.

To test the catalytic role of enzymes, we would conduct two trials of the same reaction, one with the suspected enzyme present and one without the suspected enzyme. Comparing the rate of the two reactions will prove or disprove the catalytic nature of the enzyme. If the rate of the reaction with the suspected enzyme present is faster than the rate of the control reaction, we can presume that the enzyme is catalytically active.

To test the effect of varying conditions on enzymatic activity, we again conduct two trials of the same reaction, this time with identical reactants and enzyme present. We manipulate one factor, pH, temperature, substrate concentration, or enzyme concentration, in one reaction and hold the factor constant in the control reaction. Comparing the rate of the two reactions will reveal the effect of the manipulated factor on enzyme activity.

h. Explain anabolic and catabolic pathways involved in the metabolism of macromolecules (e.g. polysaccharides, nucleic acids, proteins, lipids).

Metabolism is the sum of all the chemical changes in a cell that convert nutrients to energy and macromolecules, the complex chemical molecules important to cell structure and function. The four main classes of macromolecules are polysaccharides (carbohydrates), nucleic acids, proteins, and lipids. Metabolism consists of two contrasting processes, anabolism and catabolism. Anabolism is biosynthesis, the formation of complex macromolecules from simple precursors. Anabolic reactions require the input of energy to proceed. Catabolism is the breaking down of macromolecules obtained from the environment or cellular reserves to produce energy in the form of ATP and basic precursor molecules. The energy produced by catabolic reactions drives the anabolic pathways of the cell.

Anabolism

The anabolic pathways of a cell diverge, synthesizing a large variety of macromolecules. All anabolic reactions produce complex molecules by linking small subunits, called monomers, together to form a large unit, or polymer. The main mechanism of anabolism is condensation reactions that covalently link monomer units and release water.

Polysaccharides (carbohydrates) consist of monosaccharide units (e.g. glucose) linked together by glycosidic linkages, covalent bonds formed through condensation reactions. Glycogen is the principle storage form of glucose in animal and human cells. Cells produce glycogen by linking glucose monomers to form polymer chains.

Nucleic acids are large polymers of nucleotides. Cells link nucleotides, consisting of a five-carbon sugar, a phosphate group, and a nitrogenous base, through condensation reactions. During DNA and RNA synthesis, the template molecule dictates the sequence of nucleotides by complementary base pairing.

Proteins are large polymers of amino acid subunits called polypeptides. Cells synthesize proteins by linking amino acids, forming peptide linkages through condensation reactions. RNA sequences direct the synthesis of proteins.

Lipids are a diverse group of molecules that are hydrophobic, insoluble in water. Cells synthesize lipids from fatty acid chains formed by the addition of two-carbon units derived from a molecule called acetyl coenzyme A (acetyl-CoA). The reactions involved in lipid synthesis include condensation, oxidation/reduction, and alkylation.

Catabolism

The catabolic pathways of a cell break down macromolecules and produce energy to drive the anabolic pathways. In addition, catabolic pathways release precursor molecules (e.g. amino acids, nucleotides) used in biosynthesis. The basic reaction of catabolism is hydrolysis, the addition of a water molecule across a covalent bond.

Cells break the glycosidic linkages of stored or consumed polysaccharides, releasing glucose or other sugars that can be converted to glucose. The cells further degrade glucose to basic chemical end products, producing energy in the form of ATP.

Cells break down consumed proteins into amino acid units and other simple derivatives. Cells then use the amino acids to form new peptide chains or convert the derivative units into new amino acids. Cells can also acquire energy from the degradation of proteins, but the energy yield is not as high as that of polysaccharides and fatty acids.

Hydrolysis of lipids releases fatty acids that are a rich energy source. Fatty acids contain more than twice as much potential energy as do carbohydrates or proteins. The break down of fatty acids produces basic chemical compounds and energy in the form of ATP.

Finally, hydrolysis of nucleic acids by enzymes produces oligonucleotides (short strings of DNA or RNA) that are further degraded to produce free nucleosides (sugar-nitrogenous base units). Cells further digest nucleosides, separating the nitrogenous base from the sugar. Digestion of nucleosides ultimately results in the production of nitrogenous bases, simple sugars, and basic precursor compounds used in the synthesis of new DNA or RNA.

Skill 1.4　Integration and Control of Human Organ Systems

a. Relate the complementary activity of major body systems (e.g., circulatory, digestive, respiratory, excretory) to provide cells with oxygen and nutrients and remove waste products

All of the major body systems work in a complementary way to promote well-being. There is continuity within the body, with all systems being interconnected.

Circulatory System - The function of the circulatory system is to carry oxygenated blood and nutrients to all cells of the body and return carbon dioxide waste to be expelled from the lungs. Animals evolved from an open system to a closed system with vessels leading to and from the heart. Unoxygenated blood enters the heart through the inferior and superior vena cava. The first chamber it encounters is the right atrium. It goes through the tricuspid valve to the right ventricle, on to the pulmonary arteries, and then to the lungs where it is oxygenated. It returns to the heart through the pulmonary vein into the left atrium. It travels through the bicuspid valve to the left ventricle where it is pumped to all parts of the body through the aorta.

Digestive System - The function of the digestive system is to break down food and absorb it into the blood stream where it can be delivered to all cells of the body for use in cellular respiration. As animals evolved, digestive systems changed from simple absorption to a system with a separate mouth and anus, capable of allowing the animal to become independent of a host. The teeth and saliva begin digestion by breaking food down into smaller pieces and lubricating it so it can be swallowed. The lips, cheeks, and tongue form a bolus (ball) of food. It is carried down the pharynx by the process of peristalsis (wave like contractions) and enters the stomach through the cardiac sphincter which closes to keep food from going back up. In the stomach, pepsinogen and hydrochloric acid form pepsin, the enzyme that breaks down proteins. The food is broken down further by this chemical action and is turned into chyme. The pyloric sphincter muscle opens to allow the food to enter the small intestine. Most nutrient absorption occurs in the small intestine. Its large surface area, accomplished by its length and protrusions called villi and microvilli allow for a great absorptive surface. Upon arrival into the small intestine, chyme is neutralized to allow the enzymes found there to function. Any food left after the trip through the small intestine enters the large intestine. The large intestine functions to reabsorb water and produce vitamin K. The feces, or remaining waste, are passed out through the anus.

Respiratory System - This system functions in the gas exchange of oxygen (needed) and carbon dioxide (waste). It delivers oxygen to the bloodstream and picks up carbon dioxide for release out of the body. Simple animals diffuse gases from and to their environment. Gills allow aquatic animals to exchange gases in a fluid medium by removing dissolved oxygen from the water. Lungs maintain a fluid environment for gas exchange in terrestrial animals.

Excretory System - The function of the excretory system is to rid the body of nitrogenous wastes in the form of urea. The functional units of excretion are the nephrons, which make up the kidneys. Antidiuretic hormone (ADH), which is made in the hypothalamus and stored in the pituitary, is released when differences in osmotic balance occur. This will cause more water to be reabsorbed. As the blood becomes more dilute, ADH release ceases. Urine forms in the collecting duct which leads to the ureter then to the bladder where it is stored. Urine is passed from the bladder through the urethra. The amount of water reabsorbed back into the body is dependent upon how much water or fluids an individual has consumed. Urine can be very dilute or very concentrated if dehydration is present.

The function of the cardiovascular system is to carry oxygenated blood and nutrients to all cells of the body and return carbon dioxide waste for expulsion from the lungs. Through breathing, the respiratory system, especially the lungs, function to bind oxygen to hemoglobin. Oxygen is then carried via the circulatory system and is delivered to muscles, which rely on oxygen to contract. The respiratory system also functions by removing carbon dioxide waste. The digestive and excretory systems are also linked. The function of the digestive system is to break food down into nutrients to be absorbed into the blood stream (circulatory system) where they can be delivered to all cells of the body for use in cellular respiration. Various by-products from digestion are compacted and excreted from the body by the excretory system, and excess water is filtered by the kidneys and either reused by the body or excreted by the bladder, ureter, and urethras.

b. Explain and analyze the role of the nervous system in mediating communication between different parts of the body and the body's interactions with the environment

The human nervous system is responsible for relaying messages between the brain and body. It is comprised of two distinct parts, the central nervous system and peripheral nervous system. The **central nervous system** (CNS) consists of the brain and spinal cord. The CNS is responsible for the body's response to environmental stimuli. The spinal cord is located inside and protected by the spine. It sends out motor commands for movement in response to stimuli. The brain is where responses to more complex stimuli occurs. The meninges are the connective tissues that protect the CNS. The CNS contains fluid filled spaces called ventricles. These ventricles are filled with cerebrospinal fluid which is formed in the brain. This fluid cushions the brain and circulates nutrients, white blood cells, and hormones. The CNS's response to stimuli is a reflex. The reflex is an unconscious, automatic response. The central nervous system controls and responds to the various senses – seeing, hearing, smelling, tasting and feeling.

The **peripheral nervous system (PNS)** consists of the nerves that connect the CNS to the rest of the body. The sensory division brings information to the CNS from sensory receptors and the motor division sends signals from the CNS to effector cells. The motor division consists of the somatic nervous system and the autonomic nervous system. The somatic nervous system is controlled consciously in response to external stimuli. The large muscles of the body are controlled by the somatic nervous system. The autonomic nervous system is unconsciously controlled by the hypothalamus of the brain to regulate the internal environment. This system is responsible for the movement of smooth and cardiac muscles as well as the muscles for other organ systems. Such activities as the beating of the heart or the digestion of food are controlled by the autonomic nervous system.

Nervous System - The neuron is the basic unit of the nervous system. It consists of an axon, which carries impulses away from the cell body, the dendrite, which carries impulses toward the cell body and the cell body, which contains the nucleus. Synapses are spaces between neurons. Chemicals called neurotransmitters are found close to the synapse. The myelin sheath, composed of Schwann cells, covers the neurons and provides insulation.

c. Explain the homeostatic role of the major organs (e.g., kidneys, heart, brain)

The molecular composition of the immediate environment outside of the organism is not the same as it is inside, and the temperature outside may not be optimal for metabolic activity within the organism. **Homeostasis** is the control of these differences between internal and external environments. There are three homeostatic systems to regulate these differences, osmoregulation, excretion, and thermoregulation.

The kidneys are the site of osmoregulation. **Osmoregulation** deals with maintenance of the appropriate level of water and salts in body fluids for optimum cellular functions. The nephrons maintain osmoregulation by repeatedly filtering fluid waste and by reabsorbing water and excreting excess water. **Excretion** is the elimination of metabolic (nitrogenous) waste from the body in the form of urea. The functional unit of excretion is the nephron, many of which make up the kidneys. Sweating is also a form of excretion of fluids and some wastes.

Thermoregulation maintains the internal, or core, body temperature of the organism within a tolerable range for metabolic and cellular processes. Common indications of change in body temperature are shivering and sweating. Both are complex behaviors. Vasodilation of blood vessels close to the surface of the skin allows for cooling while vasoconstriction helps keep an organism warmer. A drop in metabolic rate, decreased heart rate, goose bumps and shivering also help keep an organism warmer. The site for thermoregulation is the hypothalamus. It is the reception site for many hormones and therefore acts as a processing area. It works with the brain to integrate nerve impulses and command activity.

d. Explain the function of feedback loops in the nervous and endocrine systems to regulate conditions in the body and predict the effects of disturbances on these systems

Feedback loops in human systems serve to regulate bodily functions in relation to environmental conditions. Positive feedback loops enhance the body's response to external stimuli and promote processes that involve rapid deviation from the initial state. For example, positive feedback loops function in stress response and the regulation of growth and development. Ovulation is controlled by a positive feedback situation. Prior to ovulation, the ovary secretes estrogen to stimulate the maturation of the ovum. The level of estrogen gives a signal to the hypothalamus and it stimulates the production of GnRH and FSH so the estrogen level will be increasing until it reaches its peak. At that time ovulation occurs. Negative feedback loops help maintain stability in spite of environmental changes and function in homeostasis. For example, negative feedback loops function in the regulation of blood glucose levels and the maintenance of body temperature. In blood glucose level regulation, the body needs glucose to create ATP, but the amounts of ATP needed fluctuates. Two hormones created in the pancreas, insulin and glucagon, regulate the concentration of glucose in the blood. The pancreas has receptors for monitoring glucose levels. When glucose levels are low, less insulin and more glucagon are released and delivered to the liver, but when glucose levels are high, more insulin and less glucagon are released to the liver. Insulin in the liver promotes the conversion of glucose into glycogen for storage. Glucagon promotes the conversion of glycogen to glucose for immediate energy needs.

A possible disturbance would be the development of diabetes mellitus due to the pancreas no longer being able to produce insulin. The body can no longer convert glucose to glycogen and the blood sugar continues to climb which can cause damage to the liver, the eyesight, and many other organs. The person with this condition has to be given insulin by shot or by mouth to regulate their blood glucose level.

e. Explain the role of hormones (e.g., digestive, reproductive, osmoregulatory) in providing internal feedback mechanisms for homeostasis at the cellular level and in whole organisms

Feedback loops often regulate the secretion of hormones in humans. The pituitary gland and hypothalamus respond to varying levels of hormones by increasing or decreasing production and secretion. High levels of a hormone cause down-regulation of the production and secretion pathways, while low levels of a hormone cause up-regulation of the production and secretion pathways.

"Fight or flight" refers to the human body's response to stress or danger. Briefly, as a response to an environmental stressor, the hypothalamus releases a hormone that acts on the pituitary gland, triggering the release of another hormone, adrenocorticotropin (ACTH), into the bloodstream. ACTH then signals the adrenal glands to release the hormones cortisol, epinephrine, and norepinephrine. These three hormones act to ready the body to respond to a threat by increasing blood pressure and heart rate, speeding reaction time, diverting blood to the muscles, and releasing glucose for use by the muscles and brain. The stress-response hormones also down-regulate growth, development, and other non-essential functions.

Finally, cortisol completes the "fight or flight" feedback loop by acting on the hypothalamus to stop hormonal production after the threat has passed.

The thyroid gland produces hormones that help maintain heart rate, blood pressure, muscle tone, digestion, and reproductive functions. The parathyroid glands maintain the calcium level in blood and the pancreas maintains glucose homeostasis by secreting insulin and glucagon. The three gonadal steroids, androgen (testosterone), estrogen, and progesterone, regulate the development of the male and female reproductive organs.

Neurotransmitters are chemical messengers. The most common neurotransmitter is acetylcholine. Acetylcholine controls muscle contraction and heartbeat. A group of neurotransmitters, the catecholamines, include epinephrine and norepinephrine. Epinephrine (adrenaline) and norepinephrine are also hormones. They are produced in response to stress. They have profound effects on the cardiovascular and respiratory systems. These hormones/neurotransmitters can be used to increase the rate and stroke volume of the heart, thus increasing the rate of oxygen delivery to the blood cells.

f. Describe the role of the musculo-skeletal system in providing structure, support, and locomotion to the human organism

The function of the muscular system is to facilitate movement. There are three types of muscle tissue: skeletal, cardiac, and smooth.

Skeletal muscle is voluntary. These muscles are attached to bones and are responsible for their movement. Skeletal muscle consists of long fibers and is striated due to the repeating patterns of the myofilaments (made of the proteins actin and myosin) that make up the fibers.

Cardiac muscle is found in the heart. Cardiac muscle is striated like skeletal muscle, but differs in that the plasma membrane of the cardiac muscle causes the muscle to beat even when away from the heart. The action potentials of cardiac and skeletal muscles also differ. A person has no direct control over cardiac muscle as he would over striated muscle.

Smooth muscle is involuntary. It is found in organs and enables functions such as digestion and respiration. Unlike skeletal and cardiac muscle, smooth muscle is not striated. Smooth muscle has less myosin and does not generate as much tension as the striated muscles. It aids with such functions as digestion by performing peristalsis.

The mechanism of skeletal muscle contraction involves a nerve impulse striking a muscle fiber. This causes calcium ions to flood the sarcomere. The myosin fibers creep along the actin, causing the muscle to contract. Once the nerve impulse has passed, calcium is pumped out and the contraction ends.

Analyze the movement of body joints

The axial skeleton consists of the bones of the skull and vertebrae. The appendicular skeleton consists of the bones of the legs, arms and tail, and shoulder girdle. Bone is a connective tissue.

Parts of the bone include compact bone which gives strength, spongy bone which contains red marrow to make blood cells, yellow marrow in the center of long bones to store fat cells, and the periosteum, which is the protective covering on the outside of the bone.

In addition to bones and muscles, ligaments and tendons are important joint components. A joint is a place where two bones meet. Joints enable movement. Ligaments attach bone to bone. Tendons attach bone to muscle. There are three types of joints:

1. Ball and socket – allow for rotational movement. An example is the joint between the shoulder and the humerus. This joint allows humans to move their arms and legs in many different ways.
2. Hinge – movement is restricted to a single plane. An example is the joint between the humerus and the ulna in the elbow.
3. Pivot – allows for the rotation of the forearm and the hands at the wrist.

Knowledge of the structure and function of the skin

The skin consists of two distinct layers. The epidermis is the thinner outer layer and the dermis is the thicker, inner layer. Layers of tightly packed epithelial cells make up the epidermis. The tight packaging of the epithelial cells supports the skin's function as a protective barrier against infection.

The top layer of the epidermis consists of dead skin cells and is filled with keratin, a waterproofing protein. The dermis layer consists of connective tissue. It contains blood vessels, hair follicles, sweat glands, and sebaceous glands. An oily secretion called sebum, produced by the sebaceous gland, is released to the outer epidermis through the hair follicles. Sebum maintains the pH of the skin between 3 and 5, which inhibits most microorganism growth.

The skin also plays a role in thermoregulation. Increased body temperature causes skin blood vessels to dilate, resulting in heat radiating from the skin's surface. The sweat glands are also activated, increasing evaporative cooling. Decreased body temperature causes skin blood vessels to constrict. This results in blood from the skin diverting to deeper tissues and reduces heat loss from the surface of the skin.

Skill 1.5 Physiology of the Immune System

The immune system is responsible for defending the body against foreign invaders. There are two defense mechanisms: non specific and specific.

The **non-specific** immune mechanism has two lines of defenses. The first lines of defense are the physical barriers of the body. These include the skin and mucous membranes. The skin prevents the penetration of bacteria and viruses as long as there are no abrasions on the skin. Hair follicles secrete sebum which conatins fatty acids and lactic acid to inhibit growth of pathogens. Mucous membranes form a protective barrier around the digestive, respiratory, and genitourinary tracts. In addition, the pH of the skin and mucous membranes inhibit the growth of many microbes. Mucous secretions (tears and saliva) wash away many microbes and contain lysozyme that kills many microbes. The lungs can expel pathogens by ciliary action working with the sneeze mechanism as well as by coughing. Most systems of the body have an acidic pH which prevents growth of bacteria.

The second line of defense includes white blood cells and the inflammatory response. **Phagocytosis** is the ingestion of foreign particles. A phagocyte is a cell which uses chemotaxis to attract, adhere to, engulf and ingest foreign bodies. Macrophages, eosinophils, and neutrophils are three types of phagocytes.

Promonocytes are made in the bone marrow and released into the blood as monocytes. Monocytes mature to become macrophages which are the largest phagocytic cells. These cells are long-lived and depend on mitochondria for energy. In some cases these cells will display proteins from previously destroyed cells on their surfaces to warn other invading cells of their fate. These cells are referred to as antigen presenting cells (APCs).

Eosinophils are also phagocytic. They can release cationic protein and perforins which burn holes in cells. Natural killer cells destroy the body's own infected cells instead of the invading the microbe directly. These cells are present in blood and lymph as large granular lymphocytes. Neutrophils make up about seventy percent of all white blood cells (leukocytes). They are phagocytes that have no mitochondria but get their energy from stored glycogen. They are short-lived, but precede the macrophages to the scene of intrusion.

There is another aspect of the inflammatory response. The blood supply to the injured area is increased, causing redness and heat. Swelling also typically occurs with inflammation. Histamine is released by basophils and mast cells when the cells are injured. This triggers the inflammatory response. Non-fixed macrophages are attracted by the histamine. They can squeeze through the walls of capillaries by diapedesis or extravasation to go to the area and destroy dead tissue or pathogens.

The **specific** immune mechanism recognizes specific foreign material and responds by destroying the invader. These mechanisms are specific and diverse. They are able to recognize individual pathogens. An **antigen** is any foreign particle that elicits an immune response, no matter if it is a bacteria or a sliver. An **antibody** is manufactured by the body and recognizes and latches onto antigens, with the intent of destroying them. They also have recognition of foreign material (non-self) versus the self. Memory of the invaders provides immunity upon further exposure.

Immunity is the body's ability to recognize and destroy an antigen before it causes harm. Active natural immunity develops after recovery from an infectious disease (e.g. chicken pox). It develops slowly but is long-term and antigen specific. Active artificial immunity develops slowly after a vaccination (e.g., mumps, measles, rubella), lasts for several years and is specific to the antigen for which the immunization was given. Passive natural immunity may be passed from one individual to another and is not permanent. A good example is the immunities passed from mother to nursing child. A baby's immune system is not well developed and the passive immunity received through nursing keeps him healthier. An injection of gamma globulin as might be given to a pregnant woman after exposure to rubella will help her develop a passive artificial immunity. The greatest advantages to this are that the immunity develops immediately and the recipient acquires immunity to all the antigens to which the donor had immunity; however, the immunity is temporary.

There are two main responses made by the body after exposure to an antigen: humoral and cell-mediated.

a. Explain the humoral response to infection

Humoral response - Free antigens activate this response and B cells (lymphocytes from bone marrow) give rise to plasma cells that secrete antibodies and memory cells that will recognize future exposures to the same antigen. T helper cells must be near the B-lymphocyte to release cytokine which helps the B-cell mature. The antibodies defend against extracellular pathogens by binding to the antigen and making it an easy target for phagocytes to engulf and destroy. Antibodies are in a class of proteins called immunoglobulins which are the gamma globulin part of blood. There are five major classes of immunoglobulins (Ig) involved in the humoral response: IgM, IgG, IgA, IgD, and IgE. IgG is responsible for the immune protection of newborns as it is the only one that can cross the placenta. IgE is responsible for autoimmune responses that include allergies, some types of arthritis, multiple sclerosis, and systemic lupus erythematosus. IgM is the main antibody of primary immune responses. IgG is the most involved in secondary immune responses. IgM is the largest of the immunoglobulins.

b. Compare cell-mediated and humoral responses to infection

The humoral response responds to an antigen and provides an established protection for future exposure. In the cell-mediated response, infected cells activate T cells (lymphocytes from the thymus). These activated T cells defend against pathogens in the cells or cancer cells by binding to the infected cell and destroying them along with the antigen. T cell receptors on the T helper cells recognize antigens bound to the body's own cells. T helper cells release IL-2 which stimulates other lymphocytes (cytotoxic T cells and B cells). Cytotoxic T cells kill infected host cells by recognizing specific antigens. Suppressor T cells inhibit the production of cytotoxic T cells when enough have been made. Memory T cells recognize and respons to a pathogen after it has once been repelled. Cell-mediated immunity is more involved with T cells while humoral response is more involved with B cells, but both B cells and T cells are used in both types of response.

c. Explain how vaccination works and distinguish among variables affecting success rate

Vaccines artificially induce immunity by priming the immune system to respond to infection by specific pathogens. Vaccines introduce antigens, proteins or polysaccharides, derived from a specific pathogen. Exposure to pathogen antigens prepares the body to respond to future infection by stimulating the production of specific antibodies and memory immune cells.

Most modern vaccines are highly successful in providing immunity to diseases. However, many variables affect the success rate of vaccination. A patient's personal characteristics and health, the type of disease and vaccine, and the method and timing of vaccination can all affect the efficacy of a vaccine.

Genetics plays an important role in the response to immunization and pathogenic invasion. Each individual responds differently to vaccines. The strength of each individual's initial immune response to a vaccine determines how well the body will respond to possible infection in the future.

Vaccines come in many different types and forms. Vaccines may consist of heat-killed viruses or bacteria such as those for flu or hepatitis A, live-attenuated (weakened) viruses or bacteria lide those for measles or mumps, subunits (e.g. single proteins) like for human papillomavirus, toxoid which are inactivate toxic compounds from the pathogen like tetanus and synthetic antigens. In addition, there are a number of new types of vaccines in development or being manufactured such as conjugate vaccines in which toxins are linked to proteins, recombinant vectors in which the microorganism and the DNA of another organism are linked, and DNA vaccination which is created from the DNA of the pathogen. Different types of vaccines are more or less effective depending on the particular disease. In addition, because different diseases require different immune responses, vaccines must stimulate the correct immunological pathways to achieve maximum success. For example, diseases caused by intracellular microbes (microbes inside host cells) are difficult to vaccinate against because they require a cell-mediated (T cell) immune response.

Historically, scientists have had greater success generating vaccines that elicit antibody responses rather than T cell responses.

The timing and method of vaccine delivery is another very important factor in the success of a vaccine. Vaccines are maximally effective when delivered on the correct schedule and at the appropriate dosage, as determined by scientific research. Many vaccines need to be delivered two or more times to boost the immunity or a booster needs to be given every few years. The medium in which the vaccine is placed and the delivery method greatly affect its effectiveness.

Finally, the health of the patient receiving the vaccine can affect the success rate. For example, studies indicate that patient stress may negatively impact the effectiveness of vaccines. Additionally, age and overall health can affect the success rates of vaccines. People with diseases like diabetes may not have immune systems that will respond correctly to the vaccine.

d. Predict the consequences of a compromised immune system [e.g., AIDS (Acquired Immune Deficiency Syndrome)]

The immune system attacks not only microbes, but also cells that are not native to the host. This is the problem with skin grafts, organ transplantations, and blood transfusions. Antibodies to foreign blood and tissue types already exist in the body. If blood is transfused that is not compatible with the host, these antibodies destroy the new blood cells. There is a similar reaction when tissue and organs are transplanted.

The major histocompatibility complex (MHC) is responsible for the rejection of tissue and organ transplants. This complex is unique to each person. Cytotoxic T cells recognize the MHC on the transplanted tissue or organ as foreign and destroy these tissues. Various drugs are needed to suppress the immune system so this does not happen. The complication with this is that the patient is now more susceptible to infection.

Autoimmune disease occurs when the body's own immune system destroys its own cells. Lupus, Grave's disease, and rheumatoid arthritis are examples of autoimmune diseases. There is no way to prevent autoimmune diseases. Immunodeficiency is a deficiency in either the humoral or cell mediated immune defenses. HIV is an example of an immunodeficiency disease.

A compromised immune system is one that is weakened by factors including age, psychological stress, poor nutrition, and diseases. People with compromised immune systems are susceptible to infection by viruses and bacteria that a healthy immune system would easily fight off. For example, AIDS patients are at increased risk of infection by normally benign viruses, intracellular bacteria, and cancers caused by viruses. Such infections require a robust T cell-mediated immune response. Because the HIV virus destroys T cells of the immune system, the immune system is unable to mount an effective immune response.

A compromised immune system often has grave consequences. The clinical manifestations of full-blown AIDS, for example, are primarily the result of increased susceptibility to opportunistic infections. The inability of the immune system to combat normally benign microbes can lead to chronic illness and eventual death.

Competency 2.0   Genetics

Skill 2.1   Chromosome Structure and Function

a. Relate the structure and function of DNA, RNA (ribonucleic acid), and proteins to the concept of variation in organisms

Proteins compose about fifty percent of the dry weight of animals and bacteria. Proteins function in structure and support (e.g., connective tissue, hair, feathers, and quills), storage of amino acids (e.g., albumin in eggs and casein in milk), transport of substances (e.g. hemoglobin), coordination body activities (e.g. insulin), signal transduction (e.g. membrane receptor proteins), contraction (e.g., muscles, cilia, and flagella), body defense (e.g. antibodies), and as enzymes to speed up chemical reactions.

All proteins are made of combinations of several of the twenty **amino acids**. An amino acid contains an amino group and an acid group. The radical group varies and defines the amino acid. Amino acids form through condensation reactions with the removal of water. The bond formed between two amino acids is called a peptide bond. Polymers of amino acids are called polypeptide chains. An analogy can be drawn between the twenty amino acids and the alphabet. We can form millions of words using an alphabet of only twenty-six letters. Similarly, organisms can create many different proteins using the twenty amino acids. This results in the formation of many different proteins, whose structure defines the function.

There are four levels of protein structure: primary, secondary, tertiary, and quaternary.

Primary structure is the protein's unique sequence of amino acids. A slight change in primary structure can affect a protein's conformation and its ability to function. **Secondary structure** is the coils and folds of polypeptide chains. The coils and folds are the result of hydrogen bonds along the polypeptide backbone. The secondary structure is either in the form of an alpha helix or a pleated sheet. The alpha helix is a coil held together by hydrogen bonds. A pleated sheet is the polypeptide chain folding back and forth. The hydrogen bonds between parallel regions hold it together. **Tertiary structure** is formed by bonding between the side chains of the amino acids. For example, disulfide bridges form when two sulfhydryl groups on the amino acids bond together to form a strong covalent bond. **Quaternary structure** is the overall structure of the protein from the aggregation of two or more polypeptide chains. An example of this is hemoglobin. Hemoglobin consists of two kinds of polypeptide chains.

Nucleic acids consist of DNA (deoxyribonucleic acid) and RNA (ribonucleic acid).

Nucleic acids contain the code for the amino acid sequence of proteins and the instructions for replicating. The monomer of nucleic acids is a nucleotide. A nucleotide consists of a 5-carbon sugar (deoxyribose in DNA, ribose in RNA), a phosphate group, and a nitrogenous base. The base sequence is the code or the instructions. There are five bases: adenine, thymine, cytosine, guanine, and uracil. Uracil is found only in RNA and replaces thymine. The following provides a summary of nucleic acid structure:

	SUGAR	PHOSPHATE	BASES
DNA	deoxy-ribose	present	adenine, thymine, cytosine, guanine
RNA	ribose	present	adenine, uracil, cytosine, guanine

Due to the molecular structure, adenine will always pair with thymine in DNA or uracil in RNA. Cytosine always pairs with guanine in both DNA and RNA.

This allows for the symmetry of the DNA molecule seen below.

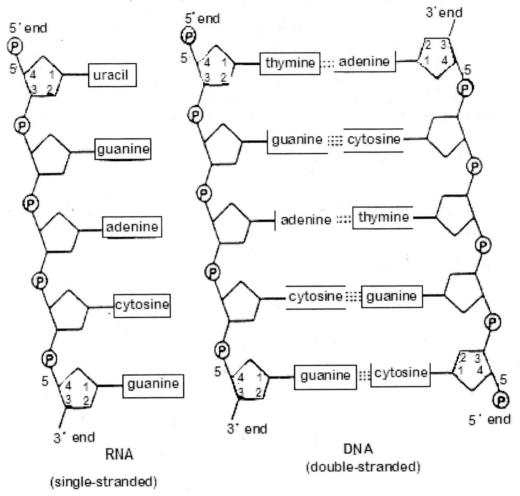

Adenine and thymine (or uracil) are linked by two covalent bonds and cytosine and guanine are linked by three covalent bonds. Guanine and cytosine are harder to break apart than thymine (uracil) and adenine because of the greater number of bonds between the bases. The double-stranded DNA molecule forms a double helix, or twisted ladder, shape.

DNA replicates semiconservatively. This means the two original strands are conserved and serve as a template for the new strand.

In DNA replication, the first step is to separate the two strands. As they separate, they unwind the supercoils to reduce tension. An enzyme called **helicase** unwinds the DNA as the replication fork proceeds and **topoisomerases** relieve the tension by nicking one strand and relaxing the supercoil.

Once the strands have separated, they must be stabilized. Single-strand binding proteins (SSBs) bind to the single strands until the DNA is replicated.

An RNA polymerase called primase adds ribonucleotides to the DNA template to initiate DNA synthesis. This short RNA-DNA hybrid is called a **primer**. Once the DNA is single stranded, **DNA polymerases** add nucleotides in the 5' → 3' direction.

As DNA synthesis proceeds along the replication fork, it becomes obvious that replication is semi-discontinuous; meaning one strand is synthesized in the direction the replication fork is moving and the other is synthesized in the opposite direction. The continuously synthesized strand is the **leading strand** and the discontinuously synthesized strand is the **lagging strand**. As the replication fork proceeds, new primer is added to the lagging strand and it is synthesized discontinuously in small fragments called **Okazaki fragments**.

The RNA primers that remain must be removed and replaced with deoxyribonucleotides. DNA polymerase has 5' → 3' polymerase activity and has 3' → 5' exonuclease activity. This enzyme binds to the nick between the Okazaki fragment and the RNA primer. It removes the primer and adds deoxyribonucleotides in the 5' → 3' direction. The nick still remains until **DNA ligase** seals it producing the final product, a double-stranded segment of DNA.

Once the double-stranded segment is replicated, there is a proofreading system carried out by DNA replication enzymes. In eukaryotes, DNA polymerases have 3' → 5' exonuclease activity—they move backwards and remove nucleotides where the enzyme recognizes an error, then add the correct nucleotide in the 5' → 3' direction. In E. coli, DNA polymerase II synthesizes DNA during repair of DNA damage.

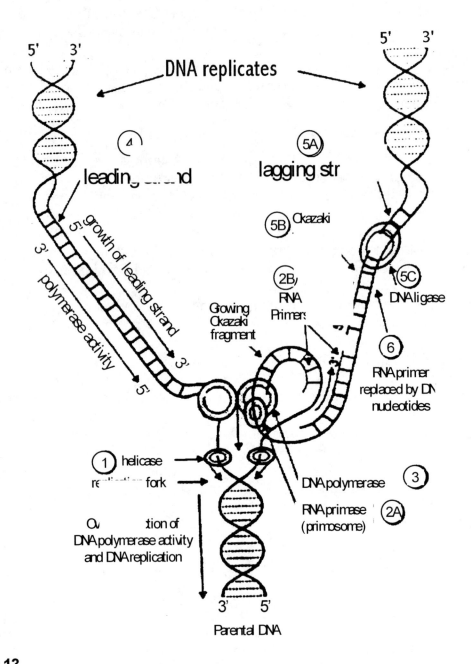

Figure 13

Chromosomal replication in bacteria is similar to eukaryotic DNA replication.

A **plasmid** is a small ring of DNA that carries accessory genes separate from those of a bacterial chromosome. Most plasmids in Gram-negative bacteria undergo bidirectional replication, although some replicate unidirectionally because of their small size. Plasmids in Gram-positive bacteria replicate by the rolling circle mechanism.

Some plasmids can transfer themselves (and therefore their genetic information) by a process called conjugation. Conjugation requires cell-to-cell contact. The sex pilus of the donor cell attaches to the recipient cell. Once contact has been established, the transfer of DNA occurs by the rolling circle mechanism.

Protein synthesis

Proteins are synthesized through the processes of transcription and translation. Three major classes of RNA are needed to carry out these processes: messenger RNA (mRNA), ribosomal RNA (rRNA), transfer RNA (tRNA). **Messenger RNA** contains information for translation. **Ribosomal RNA** is a structural component of the ribosome and **transfer RNA** carries amino acids to the ribosome for protein synthesis.

Transcription is similar in prokaryotes and eukaryotes. During transcription, the DNA molecule is copied into an RNA molecule (mRNA). Transcription occurs through the steps of initiation, elongation, and termination. Transcription also occurs for rRNA and tRNA, but the focus here is on mRNA.

Initiation begins at the promoter of the double-stranded DNA molecule. The promoter is a specific region of DNA that directs the **RNA polymerase** to bind to the DNA. The double-stranded DNA opens up and RNA polymerase begins transcription in the 5' → 3' direction by pairing ribonucleotides to the deoxyribonucleotides as follows to get a complementary mRNA segment:

Deoxyribonucleotide		Ribonucleotide
A	→	U
G	→	C

Elongation is the synthesis on the mRNA strand in the 5' → 3' direction. The new mRNA rapidly separates from the DNA template and the complementary DNA strands pair together.

Termination of transcription occurs at the end of a gene. Cleavage occurs at specific sites on the mRNA. This process is aided by termination factors.

In eukaryotes, mRNA goes through **posttranscriptional processing** before going on to **translation**.

There are three basic steps of processing:

1. **5' capping** – The addition of a base with a methyl attached to it that protects the 5' end from degradation and serves as the site where ribosomes bind to the mRNA for translation.

2. **3' polyadenylation** – The addition of 100-300 adenines to the free 3' end of mRNA resulting in a poly-A-tail.

3. **Intron removal**- The removal of non-coding introns and the splicing together of coding exons are to form the mature mRNA.

Translation is the process in which the mRNA sequence becomes a polypeptide. The mRNA sequence determines the amino acid sequence of a protein by following a pattern called the genetic code. The **genetic code** consists of 64 triplet nucleotide combinations called **codons**. Three codons are termination codons and the remaining 61 code for amino acids. There are 20 amino acids mRNA codes for. Amino acids are the building blocks of protein. They are attached together by peptide bonds to form a polypeptide chain.

Ribosomes are the site of translation. They contain rRNA and many proteins. Translation occurs in three steps: initiation, elongation, and termination. Initiation occurs when the methylated tRNA binds to the ribosome to form a complex. This complex then binds to the 5' cap of the mRNA. In elongation, tRNAs carry the amino acid to the ribosome and place it in order according to the mRNA sequence. tRNA is very specific – it only accepts one of the 20 amino acids that corresponds to the anticodon. The anticodon is complementary to the codon. For example, using the codon sequence below:

the mRNA reads A U G / G A G / C A U / G C U
the anticodons are U A C / C U C / G U A / C G A

Termination occurs when the ribosome reaches any one of the three stop codons: UAA, UAG, or UGA. The newly formed polypeptide then undergoes posttranslational modification to alter or remove portions of the polypeptide.

b. Describe chromosome structure as a sequence of genes each with a specific locus

Chromosomes are the physical structures found in every cell that carry the genetic information (DNA) of an organism and function in the transmission of hereditary information. Each chromosome contains a sequence of genes each with a specific locus. A locus is the position a given gene occupies on a chromosome. Each gene consists of a sequence of DNA that dictates a particular characteristic of an organism. Separating the genes on a chromosome are regions of DNA that do not code for proteins or other cellular products, but may function in the regulation of coding regions.

Skill 2.2   Patterns of Inheritance

a. Explain the necessity of both meiosis and fertilization in promoting variation

Meiosis and fertilization are responsible for genetic diversity. There are several mechanisms that contribute to genetic variation in sexual reproductive organisms. Three of them are independent assortment of chromosomes, crossing over, and random fertilization.

At the metaphase I stage of meiosis, each homologous pair of chromosomes is situated along the metaphase plate. The orientation of the homologous pairs is random and independent of the other pairs of chromosomes in metaphase I. This results in an **independent assortment** of maternal and paternal chromosomes. Based on this information, it seems as though each chromosome in a gamete would be of only maternal or paternal origin. A process called crossing over prevents this from happening.

Crossing over occurs during prophase I. At this point, nonsister chromatids cross and exchange corresponding segments. Crossing over results in the combination of DNA from both parents, allowing for greater genetic variation in sexual life cycles.

Random fertilization also results in genetic variation. Each parent has about 8 million possible chromosome combinations. This allows for over 60 trillion diploid combinations.

b. Describe the role of chromosomes in determining phenotypes (e.g., sex determination, chromosomal aberrations)

Each chromosome, of which there are 46 (2 pairs of 23) in humans, is home to genes. Genes are the unit of inheritance. In humans, chromosomal crossing over determines the sex of the individual. A woman's sex is denoted as XX, so she always donates an X chromosome to her child. The male sex is determined by XY, so the father can pass on either an X or Y chromosome to his offspring. It is the paring of maternal and paternal genes that determines the sex of the baby. It is also true that a parent passes on other genes affecting phenotype such as eye color, height, and physique. Chromosomal aberrations, changes in either the total number of chromosomes or their shape and size, may lead to abnormalities in the offspring. For example, an aberration on chromosome 21 causes Down syndrome.

The actual information on the genes is the genotype of an organism, but how that information is expressed outwardly is the phenotype. For example, humans have many phenotypic variations in eye color. There are two major genes and several minor genes that account for the great variety of eye colorations.

c. Predict the probable outcome of phenotypes in a genetic cross from the genotypes of the parents and mode of inheritance (e.g., autosomal or X-linked, dominant or recessive, codominance)

Based on Mendelian genetics, the more complex hereditary pattern of **dominance** was discovered. In Mendel's law of segregation, the parents have a genotype of PP for purple and pp for white, so the F_1 generation have either purple (both PP and Pp genotypes give phenotypes of purple) or white flowers which come from the pp genotype. This is an example of **complete dominance**.

Incomplete dominance is when the F_1 generation results in an appearance somewhere between the two parents. For example, red flowers (RR) are crossed with white flowers (rr), resulting in an F_1 generation with pink flowers (Rr) as well as red flowers (RR) and white flowers (rr). The red and white traits are still carried by the F_1 generation, resulting in an F_2 generation with a phenotypic ratio of 1:2:1, or 1 red:;2 pink:1white. In this situation, the genotype and phenotype are the same.

In **codominance**, the genes may form new phenotypes. The ABO blood grouping is an example of codominance. A and B are of equal strength and O is recessive. Therefore, type A blood may have the genotypes of AA or AO, type B blood may have the genotypes of BB or BO, type AB blood has the genotype A and B, and type O blood has two recessive O genes.

In humans, each cell contains 23 pairs of chromosomes, for a total of 46. Twenty-two of these pairs, called autosomes, are the same in males and females. The last pair, the sex chromosomes, differ. Females have two copies of the X chromosome, while males have one X and one Y chromosome. There are specific genes located on the sex chromosomes that are responsible for specific actions. These are called sex-linked traits. An example is hemophilia, which is determined by a gene defect on an X chromosome. If the mother carries the trait on one of her X chromosomes, she will not be a hemophiliac because her other X chromosome is normal. However, if she donates this defective X chromosome to a son who has a Y chromosome rather than a normal X chromosome, he will be a hemophiliac. If she donates the defective X chromosome to a daughter and the father donates a normal X to the daughter, the daughter will be a carrier.

d. Explain the genetic and cellular bases for Mendel's laws of dominance, segregation, and independent assortment

Gregor Mendel is recognized as the father of genetics. His work in the late 1800's is the basis of our knowledge of genetics. Although unaware of the presence of DNA or genes, Mendel realized there were factors (now known as **genes**) that were transferred from parents to their offspring. Mendel worked with pea plants and pollinated the plants himself, keeping track of subsequent generations which led to the Mendelian laws of genetics. Mendel found that two "factors" governed each trait, one from each parent. Traits or characteristics came in several forms, known as **alleles**. For example, the trait of flower color had white alleles (*pp*) and purple alleles (*PP*). Mendel formulated two laws: the law of segregation and the law of independent assortment.

The **law of segregation** states that only one of the two possible alleles from each parent is passed on to the offspring. If the two alleles differ, then one is fully expressed in the organism's appearance (the dominant allele) and the other has no noticeable effect on appearance (the recessive allele). The two alleles for each trait segregate into different gametes. A Punnet square can be used to show the law of segregation. In a Punnet square, one parent's genes are put at the top of the box and the other parent's on the side. Genes combine in the squares just like numbers are added in addition tables. This Punnet square shows the result of the cross of two F_1 hybrids.

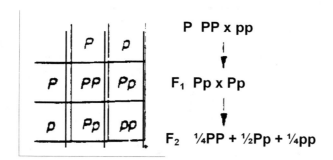

This cross results in a 1:2:1 ratio of F_2 offspring (1 PP:2 Pp:1pp). Here, the *P* is the dominant allele and the *p* is the recessive allele. The F_1 cross produces three offspring with the dominant allele expressed (two *PP* and one *Pp*) and one offspring with the recessive allele expressed (*pp*). Some other important terms to know:

Homozygous – having a pair of identical alleles. For example, *PP* and *pp* are homozygous pairs.
Heterozygous – having two different alleles. For example, *Pp* is a heterozygous pair.
Phenotype – the organism's physical appearance.
Genotype – the organism's genetic makeup. For example, *PP* and *Pp* genotypes have the same phenotype (purple in color)..

The **law of independent assortment** states that alleles assort independently of each other. The law of segregation applies for monohybrid crosses (only one character, in this case flower color, is experimented with). In a dihybrid cross, two characters are explored. Two of the seven characters Mendel studied were seed shape and color. Yellow is the dominant seed color (Y) and green is the recessive color (y). The dominant seed shape is round (R) and the recessive shape is wrinkled (r). A cross between a plant with yellow round seeds ($YYRR$) and a plant with green wrinkled seeds ($yyrr$) produces an F_1 generation with the genotype $YyRr$. The production of F_2 offspring results in a 9:3:3:1 phenotypic ratio. The yellow alleles assort separately from the round or wrinkled alleles just as the round and wrinkled alleles are independent of the green alleles.

Mendel was very lucky in choosing a plant whose traits were passed on and expressed as dominant and recessive rather than codominant. His peas had dominant phenotypes if they were genotypically homozygous or heterozygous for the dominant allele and recessive phenotypes if they were genotypically homozygous in regard to the recessive allele.

F_2

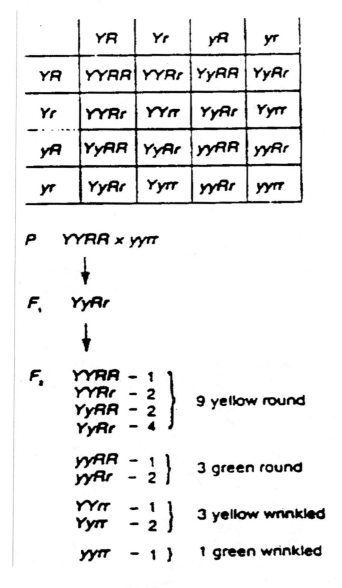

	YR	Yr	yR	yr
YR	YYRR	YYRr	YyRR	YyRr
Yr	YYRr	YYrr	YyRr	Yyrr
yR	YyRR	YyRr	yyRR	yyRr
yr	YyRr	Yyrr	yyRr	yyrr

P   YYRR x yyrr

F₁   YyRr

F₂
YYRR - 1 ⎫
YYRr - 2 ⎬ 9 yellow round
YyRR - 2 ⎪
YyRr - 4 ⎭

yyRR - 1 ⎫ 3 green round
yyRr - 2 ⎬

YYrr - 1 ⎫ 3 yellow wrinkled
Yyrr - 2 ⎬

yyrr - 1 } 1 green wrinkled

Skill 2.3   Gene Expression

a. Explain how random chromosome segregation explains the probability that a particular allele will be in a gamete

The **law of segregation** states that only one of the two possible alleles from each parent is passed on to the offspring. If the two alleles differ, then one is fully expressed in the organism's appearance (the dominant allele) and the other has no noticeable effect on appearance (the recessive allele). The two alleles for each trait segregate into different gametes. There is a 50/50 chance that each allele could be segregated into a particular gamete.

b. Recognize that specialization of cells in multicellular organisms is usually due to different patterns of gene expression rather than to differences among the genes themselves

Different cell types in a multicellular organism are dramatically different in terms of function and structure. Although two cells may look and function differently within the organism, it is important to note that an organism's cells contain the same genome. Cellular specialization generally depends on changes in gene expression rather than on different genes being present. Cell types in a multicellular organism are different from one another because of the synthesis of RNA and protein molecules. This occurs without alteration to the sequence of DNA. Let us look at control of gene expression, to see how the same genome can be presented differently. In bacterial cells, the *lac* operon is a good example of the control of gene expression. The *lac* operon contains the genes that code for the enzymes used to convert lactose into fuel (glucose and galactose). The *lac* operon contains three genes, *lac Z*, *lac Y*, and *lac A*. *Lac Z* codes for an enzyme that converts lactose into glucose and galactose. *Lac Y* codes for an enzyme that causes lactose to enter the cell. *Lac A* codes for an enzyme that acetylates lactose.

The *lac* operon also contains a promoter and an operator that is the "off and on" switch for the operon. A protein called the repressor switches the operon off when it binds to the operator. When lactose is absent, the repressor is active and the operon is turned off. The operon is turned on again when allolactose (formed from lactose) inactivates the repressor by binding to it.

c. Describe how alleles that are lethal in a homozygous individual may be carried in a heterozygote and thus maintained in a gene pool

Because of the existence of dominant and recessive alleles, individuals may exist in a population as carriers without any outward signs of disease. For example, Cystic Fibrosis (CF) is a common hereditary disease. CF is caused by a mutation in a gene called the cystic fibrosis transmembrane conductance regulator (CFTR). This gene helps create sweat, digestive juices, and mucus. Although most people without CF have two working copies of the CFTR gene, a minimum of one is needed to prevent cystic fibrosis. CF develops when neither gene works normally. CF is considered an autosomal recessive disease. If a child inherits both recessive non-functioning genes from its parents, it will be a homozygous recessive individual and the result will be CF. CF affects the entire body, causing progressive disability and early death. The test for diagnosis is a sweat test that assesses the level of chloride secreted by the body. Symptoms of CF include difficulty breathing, sinus infections, poor growth, and diarrhea. CF is one of the most common fatal inherited diseases. It is most prevalent among Caucasians; one in every 25 people of European descent carries one gene for CF.

Interestingly, most adult carriers are not aware that they are carriers and live long, healthy lives. Individuals with cystic fibrosis can be diagnosed prior to birth by genetic testing or in early childhood by a sweat test.

d. Distinguish when and why mutations in the DNA sequence of a gene may or may not affect the expression of the gene or the sequence of amino acids in an encoded protein

Inheritable changes in DNA are called mutations. **Mutations** may be errors in replication or a spontaneous rearrangement of one or more segments by factors like radioactivity, drugs, or chemicals. The severity of the change is not as critical as where the change occurs. DNA contains large segments of non-coding areas called introns. The important coding areas are called exons. If an error occurs on an intron, there is no effect. If the error occurs on an exon, it may be minor to lethal depending on the severity of the mistake. Mutations may occur on somatic or sex cells. Usually the mutations on sex cells are more dangerous since they contain the basis of all information for the developing offspring. But mutations are not always bad. They are the basis of evolution and if they create a favorable variation that enhances the organism's survival they are beneficial. But mutations may also lead to abnormalities, birth defects, and even death. There are several types of mutations.

A **point mutation** is a mutation involving a single nucleotide or a few adjacent nucleotides. Let's suppose a normal sequence was as follows:

Normal:	A B C D E F
Duplication - one nucleotide is repeated	A B **C C** D E F
Inversion - a segment of the sequence is flipped around	A **E D C B** F
Deletion - a nucleotide is left out	A B C E F
	(D is lost)
Insertion or **Translocation** - a segment from another place on the DNA is stuck in the wrong place	A B C **R S** D E F
Breakage - a piece is lost	A B C (DEF is lost)

Deletion and insertion mutations that shift the reading frame are **frame shift mutations**.

A **silent mutation** makes no change in the amino acid sequence, therefore it does not alter the protein function. A **missense mutation** results in an alteration in the amino acid sequence. A mutation's effect on protein function depends on which amino acids are involved and how many are involved. The structure of a protein usually determines its function. A mutation that does not alter the structure will probably have little or no effect on the protein's function. However, a mutation that does alter the structure of a protein and can severely affect protein activity is called a **loss-of-function mutation**. Sickle-cell anemia and cystic fibrosis are examples of loss-of-function mutations.

Skill 2.4   Biotechnology

a. Recognize how genetic engineering (biotechnology) produces biomedical and agricultural products

Genetic engineering has made enormous contributions to medicine and has opened the door to DNA technology.

The use of DNA probes and the polymerase chain reaction (PCR) has enabled scientists to identify and detect elusive pathogens. Diagnosis of genetic disease is now possible before the onset of symptoms.

Genetic engineering has allowed for the treatment of some genetic disorders. **Gene therapy** is the introduction of a normal allele to the somatic cells to replace the defective allele. The medical field has had success in treating patients with a single enzyme deficiency disease. Gene therapy has allowed doctors and scientists to introduce a normal allele that would provide the missing enzyme.

Insulin and mammalian growth hormones have been produced in bacteria by gene-splicing techniques. Insulin treatment helps control diabetes for millions of people who suffer from the disease. The insulin produced in genetically engineered bacteria is chemically identical to that made in the pancreas. Human growth hormone (HGH) has been genetically engineered for treatment of dwarfism caused by insufficient amounts of HGH. HGH is being further researched for treatment of broken bones and severe burns.

Biotechnology has advanced the techniques used to create vaccines. Genetic engineering allows for the modification of a pathogen in order to attenuate it for vaccine use. In fact, vaccines created by a pathogen attenuated by gene-splicing may be safer than those that use the traditional mutants.

Forensic scientists regularly use DNA technology to solve crimes. DNA testing can determine a person's guilt or innocence. A suspect's DNA is compared to the DNA found at the crime scene. If the DNA matches, guilt can then be established.

Biotechnology has benefited agriculture also. For example, many dairy cows are given bovine growth hormone to increase milk production. Commercially grown plants are often genetically modified for optimal growth.

Strains of wheat, cotton, and soybeans have been developed to resist herbicides used to control weeds. This allows for the successful growth of the plants while destroying the weeds. Varieties can be genetically engineered to be disease-resistant, drought-resistant, stronger, and/or give a greater yield.

Crop plants are also being engineered to resist infections and pests. Scientists can genetically modify crops to contain a viral gene that does not affect the plant and will "vaccinate" the plant from a virus attack. Crop plants are now being modified to resist insect attacks. This allows farmers to reduce the amount of pesticide used on plants.

b. Describe the construction of recombinant DNA molecules by basic DNA technology including restriction digestion by endonucleases, gel electrophoresis, ligation, and transformation

In its simplest form, genetic engineering requires enzymes to cut DNA, a vector, and a host organism for the recombinant DNA. A **restriction enzyme** is a bacterial enzyme that cuts foreign DNA in specific locations. The restriction fragment that results can be inserted into a bacterial plasmid **(vector)**. Other vectors that may be used include viruses and bacteriophages. The splicing of restriction fragments into a plasmid results in a recombinant plasmid. This recombinant plasmid can then be placed in a host cell, usually a bacterial cell, for replication.

The use of recombinant DNA provides a means to transplant genes among species. This opens the door for cloning specific genes of interest. Hybridization can be used to find a gene of interest. A probe is a molecule complementary in sequence to the gene of interest. The probe, once it has bonded to the gene, can be detected by labeling with a radioactive isotope or a fluorescent tag.

Gel electrophoresis is another method for analyzing DNA. Electrophoresis separates DNA or protein by size or electrical charge. The DNA runs towards the positive charge and the DNA fragments separate by size. The gel is treated with a DNA-binding dye that fluoresces under ultraviolet light. A picture of the gel can be taken and used for analysis.

One of the most widely used genetic engineering techniques is the **polymerase chain reaction (PCR)**. PCR is a technique in which a piece of DNA can be amplified into billions of copies within a few hours. This process requires a primer to specify the segment to be copied, and an enzyme (usually taq polymerase) to amplify the DNA. PCR has allowed scientists to perform multiple procedures on small amounts of DNA.

Skill 2.5   Bioethics

a. Discuss issues of bioethics including genetic engineering, cloning, the human genome project, gene therapy, and medical implications

Genetic engineering is the term used to describe the process of manipulating genetic information.

The goal is to introduce new attributes that are deemed to be an improvement. Often this utility is used to make a crop resistant to an herbicide, introduce a novel trait, or produce a new protein/enzyme. Examples include the production of human insulin through modified bacteria and the production of new strains of experimental mice such as the 'Oncomouse' (cancer mouse) for research. It is common for genetically engineered items to be of practical or medicinal use to humans.

Cloning is the duplication of genetic information. A clone is directly copied from another living being, and is therefore identical to its parent organism. Occasionally this process happens in nature by chance, such as the creation of identical twins. Clones are also created naturally when an organism's regular mode of reproduction is asexual. In recent years the term cloning most often refers to the intentional, not naturally occurring, production of a living organism genetically identical to its donor. Cloning is an interesting debate topic. From a scientific point of view, cloning allows us to create a "safety-blanket individual", while others argue that we are replicating creation, which many feel is a clear breach of ethical boundaries. Through cloning, scientists have created many mammals, including sheep, monkeys, cattle, horses, cats, and dogs, in their laboratories. One of the common arguments made by conservative religious groups is that the use of embryonic cells in cloning is unethical. Others believe that cloning is a slippery slope; that procreation will turn into manufacture.

The goal of the human genome project is to map and sequence the three billion nucleotides in the human genome, and to identify all of the genes on it. The project was launched in 1986 and an outline of the genome was finished in 2000 through international collaboration. In May 2006, the sequence of the last chromosome was published. While the map and sequencing are complete, scientists are still studying the functions of all the genes and their regulation. Humans have successfully decoded the genome of other mammals as well. Gene therapy is another area of current interest. Gene therapy is the addition of genes into an individual's cells/tissues to treat a disease. Often, gene therapy aims to supplement or replace a defective allele with a functional one. Advances in the human genome project have led to a greater understanding of the functions of specific genes. This has led, for example, to the formation of insulin via a bacterial vector, which can then be injected into diabetic people who cannot produce it naturally.

Gene therapy is still in its early years as far as technology goes. It is a short-lived solution because after insertion the target cells must remain functional and the cells containing the therapeutic DNA must be long-lived and stable. Patients presently have to undergo multiple rounds of gene therapy, an exhaustive and expensive prospect. In addition, there is always the risk for an inflammatory response. Anytime a foreign object is introduced into human tissues, the immune system will attack the invader, even if the invader's intention is helpful.

Genetic engineering has drastically advanced the area of biotechnology. With these advancements come concerns about safety and ethics. Many safety concerns have been answered by strict government regulations. The FDA, USDA, EPA, and National Institutes of Health are just a few of the government agencies that regulate pharmaceutical, food, and environmental technology advancements.

Several ethical questions arise when discussing biotechnology. Should embryonic stem cell research be allowed? Is animal testing humane? These are just a couple of ethical questions that many people have. There are strong arguments for both sides of the issues and there are some government regulations in place to monitor these issues.

Competency 3.0   Evolution

Skill 3.1   Natural Selection

a. Explain why natural selection acts on the phenotype rather than the genotype of an organism

Natural selection is based on the survival of certain traits in a population through the course of time.   The phrase "survival of the fittest," is often associated with natural selection. Fitness is the contribution an individual makes to the gene pool of the next generation.

Natural selection acts on phenotypes. An organism's phenotype is constantly exposed to its environment. The expressed traits, or phenotype, either help the organism to survive or in some way make its survival less likely. Based on an organism's phenotype, selection indirectly adapts a population to its environment by maintaining favorable genotypes in the gene pool.

There are three modes of natural selection. **Stabilizing selection** favors the more common phenotypes, **directional selection** shifts the frequency of phenotypes in one direction, and **diversifying selection** favors individuals on both extremes of the phenotypic range.

b. Predict the survival potential of various groups of organisms based on the amount of diversity in their gene pools

Diversity aids a population by providing possible improvements and increasing the chances of survival in changing conditions. If an organism is born with a favorable trait, it will survive and prosper. Mates will be attracted to individuals with favorable characteristics and the favorable allele will multiply through offspring and successive generations. Populations change because of the survival of a few, select individuals who preferentially reproduce, not from the gradual change of all individuals in the population. Spontaneous mutations and recessive alleles provide continued diversity. The more diversity there is within a group, the more possibilities exist for improvement. Increased diversity also gives more individuals a chance to survive if the climate changes or if there is a change in the number or types of the predators of the species or the amount or type of prey available for the species to eat. Therefore, while mutations are sometimes fatal, for those organisms with favorable mutations/genotypes/phenotypes, survival increases linearly with diversity. Populations lacking diversity are at risk of extinction.

Skill 3.2   Evolutionary Patterns

a. Analyze fossil evidence with regard to biological diversity, episodic speciation, and mass extinction.

The fossil record is a rich source of evidence and information for the study of biological diversity, episodic speciation, and mass extinction.

Life on Earth is tremendously diverse and diversity continues to increase with time. Despite this colossal diversity, many seemingly unrelated species display a surprisingly large amount of structural similarity. For example, the skeletons of mice and humans are very similar. Such similarity between species indicates descent from a common ancestor, whose existence we can often confirm by studying the fossil record. In addition, evolutionary theory explains that biological diversity results from the adaptations of native or migrant predecessors to changing environments. Thus, the fossil record should provide evidence of common ancestors or proof of migration. And, in fact, studies of fossil layers indicate that the diversity and complexity of species has increased over time.

When studying the fossil record for evidence of evolution, biologists have noted that there are many gaps between species in suspected lineages. Biologists use the episodic nature of speciation to explain gaps in the fossil record. Gaps in the fossil record may indicate that evolution proceeds intermittently, not in a strictly gradual way. Small changes in a lineage that lead to eventual reproductive isolation and speciation may not show up in the fossil record. Thus, the changes in lineages seen in the fossil record are often the result of episodic speciation events.

Finally, scientists define a mass extinction event as a brief period where a large number of species become extinct. The fossil record indicates that there have been between five and fifteen mass extinction events in the Earth's history. Scientists look for the disappearance of multiple species from the fossil record during a single time period as evidence of a mass extinction event. This method of identification can be misleading, however, because other factors such as environmental changes can artificially erase species from the fossil record.

b. Analyze the effects of evolutionary patterns on the diversity of organisms (e.g., genetic drift, convergent evolution, punctuated equilibrium, patterns of selection)

There are two theories on the rate of evolution. **Gradualism** is the theory that minor evolutionary changes occur at a regular rate. Darwin's book, "On the Origin of Species," is based on this theory of gradualism.

Charles Darwin was born in 1809 and spent 5 years in his twenties on a ship called the *Beagle*. Of all the locations the *Beagle* sailed to, it was the Galapagos Islands that infatuated Darwin. There he collected 13 species of finches that were quite similar. He could not accurately determine whether these finches were of the same species. He later learned these finches were in fact separate species.

Darwin began to hypothesize that a new species arose from its ancestors by the gradual collection of adaptations to a different environment. Darwin's most popular hypothesis involves the beak size of Galapagos finches. He theorized that the finches' beak sizes evolved to accommodate different food sources. Many people did not believe in Darwin's theories until recent field studies proved successful.

Although Darwin believed the origin of species was gradual, he was bewildered by the gaps in fossil records of living organisms. **Punctuated equilibrium** is the model of evolution that states that organismal form diverges and species form rapidly over relatively short periods of geological history, and then progress through long stages of stasis with little or no change. Punctuationalists use fossil records to support their claim. It is probable that both gradualism and punctuated equilibrium are correct, depending on the particular lineage studied.

Genetic drift is, along with natural selection, one of the main mechanisms of evolution. Genetic drift refers to the chance deviation in the frequency of alleles (traits) resulting from the randomness of zygote formation and selection. Because only a small percentage of all possible zygotes become mature adults, parents do not necessarily pass all of their alleles on to their offspring. Genetic drift is particularly important in small populations because chance deviations in allelic frequency can quickly alter the genotypic make-up of the population. In extreme cases, certain alleles may completely disappear from the gene pool. Genetic drift is particularly influential when environmental events and conditions produce small, isolated populations. The loss of traits associated with genetic drift in small populations can decrease genetic diversity.

Convergent evolution describes the process of organisms developing similar characteristics while evolving in different locations or ecosystems. Such organisms do not descend from a common ancestor, but develop similar characteristics because they react and adapt to environmental pressures in the same way. Thus, convergent evolution reduces biological diversity by making distinct species more like each other.

Punctuated equilibrium is the model of evolution that states that organismal forms diverge, and species form, rapidly over relatively short periods. Between the times of rapid speciation, the characteristics of species are relatively stable. Punctuationalists use fossil records to support their claim. Punctuated equilibrium affects the diversity of organisms in two ways. First, during the period of rapid change and speciation, the diversity of organisms increases dramatically. Second, during the intervening periods, the diversity of organisms remains nearly unchanged.

Patterns of selection are the effects of selection on phenotypes. The four main patterns of selection are stabilizing, disruptive, directional, and balancing. Stabilizing selection is the selection against extreme values of a trait and selection for the average or intermediate values. Conversely, disruptive selection favors individuals at both extremes of the distribution of a characteristic or trait, while directional selection progressively favors one extreme of a characteristic distribution. Finally, balancing selection maintains multiple alleles in a population, often by favoring heterozygote individuals. Balancing selection is the only pattern of selection that increases genetic diversity. Stabilizing, disruptive, and directional selection all work to decrease diversity by totally eliminating unfavorable characteristics from the population.

c. Explain the conditions for Hardy-Weinberg equilibrium and why they are unlikely to appear in nature, and solve equations to predict the frequency of genotypes in a population

Evolution currently is defined as a change in genotype over time. Gene frequencies shift and change from generation to generation. Populations evolve, not individuals. The **Hardy-Weinberg** theory of gene equilibrium is a mathematical prediction to show shifting gene patterns. Let's use the letter "A" to represent the dominant condition of normal skin pigment, and the letter "a" to represent the recessive condition of albinism. In a population, there are three possible genotypes: *AA, Aa* and *aa*. *AA* and *Aa* would have normal skin pigment and only *aa* would be albinos.

According to the Hardy-Weinberg law, there are five requirements that keep gene frequency stable and limit evolution:

1. There is no mutation in the population.
2. There are no selection pressures; one gene is not more desirable in the environment.
3. There is no mating preference; mating is random.
4. The population is isolated; there is no immigration or emigration.
5. The population is large (mathematical probability is more correct with a large sample).

The above conditions are extremely difficult to meet. If these five conditions are not met, then gene frequency can shift, leading to evolution. Let's say in a population, 75% of the population has normal skin pigment (*AA* and *Aa*) and 25% are albino (*aa*). Using the following formula, we can determine the frequency of the *A* allele and the *a* allele in a population.

This formula can be used over generations to determine if evolution is occurring. The formula is: $1 = p^2 + 2pq + q^2$; where 1 is the total population, p^2 is the number of *AA* individuals, $2pq$ is the number of *Aa* individuals, and q^2 is the number of *aa* individuals.

Since you cannot tell by looking if an individual is *AA* or *Aa*, you must use the *aa* individuals to find that frequency first. As stated above *aa* was 25% of the population. Since $aa = q^2$, we can determine the value of q (or a) by finding the square root of 0.25, which is 0.5. Therefore, 0.5 of the population has the *a* gene. In order to find the value for p, use the following formula: $1 = p + q$. This would make the value of $p = 0.5$.

The gene pool is all the alleles at all gene loci in all individuals of a population. The Hardy-Weinberg theorem describes the gene pool in a non-evolving population. It states that the frequencies of alleles and genotypes in a population's gene pool are random unless acted on by something other than sexual recombination.

Now, to find the number of *AA*, plug it into the first formula:

$$AA = p^2 = 0.5 \times 0.5 = 0.25$$
$$Aa = 2pq = 2(0.5 \times 0.5) = 0.5$$
$$aa = q^2 = 0.5 \times 0.5 = 0.25$$

Any problem you may have with Hardy-Weinberg will have an obvious squared number. The square of that number will be the frequency of the recessive gene, and you can figure anything else out knowing the formula and the frequency of q.

When frequencies vary from the Hardy-Weinberg equilibrium, the population is evolving. The change to the gene pool is on such a small scale that it is called microevolution. Certain factors increase the chances of variability in a population, thus leading to evolution. Items that increase variability include mutations, sexual reproduction, immigration, large population, and variation in geographic locale. Changes that decrease variation are natural selection, emigration, small population, and random mating.

Skill 3.3   Mechanisms for Speciation

a. Distinguish between the accommodation of an individual organism to its environment and the gradual adaptation of a lineage of organisms through genetic change

An organism may be forced to adapt to a changed environment. When it is forced to do this, its behavior is modified, but its genotype remains unchanged. However, a certain individual may be born within that population and may have a genotype that is favorable under the new conditions. Survival of the fittest then demands that the individual with the favorable trait will be more likely to survive and reproduce. The offspring of the more fit individual will then carry forward the favorable genotype. Over time, as the individuals with the favored genotype reproduce, the population is gradually shifted so that more organisms exist with the favorable trait.

Homology is any similarity between characteristics due to shared ancestry. Anatomical structures that perform the same function in different biological species and evolved from the same structure in some ancestor species are homologous. This homology can also be seen in the DNA of the two species. An example would be the wings of bats and the arms of humans. It can also refer to structures that arose from the same tissue in embryonic development such as the ovaries of females and the testicles of males.

The wings of a maple seed and the wings of a bat are analogous but not homologous in that they both help the organism to travel by wind but they did not develop from the same structure. Some structures are both homologous and analogous like the wings of a bat and the wings of a robin. In evolution, the bat and the robin may have evolved through different lineages (initially divergent), but they both had forelimbs that developed the same function so that the evolution became convergent with the structures analogous.

b. Describe a scenario that demonstrates the effects of reproductive or geographic isolation on speciation

Isolation of a population, whether by reproductive or geographic means, can cause speciation. If a population is separated by a geographical boundary, for example the formation of a mountain range or the separation of the supercontinent Pangaea, the population could usually still breed if they were to make contact again. This is strictly a case of the species remaining the same and individuals being physically separated. Geographic isolation is also known as allopatry. Occasionally, if the environment changes, the survival of the fittest model may act upon a population causing the formation of a separate species. When this occurs, even if reintroduced, the populations will have unsuccessful mating encounters.

Reproductive isolation prevents two or more populations from exchanging genes. Reproductive isolation can occur by preventing fertilization, or by the genesis of a degenerate or sterile hybrid, such as the common mule. Pre-zygotic barriers to fertilization include a physical barrier (such as an ocean) to errors in cell division that cause incompatibility between populations. If fertilization does occur, several other barriers exist. Spontaneous abortion of the fetus is likely to occur. For a hybrid that has been born, it is probable that the hybrid will be sterile and produce no offspring of its own. Sterility and death before developing into sexual maturity help to ensure that hybrid genes are not passed on. Finally, hybrids that do produce offspring can, potentially, produce sterile progeny.

It is more common for there to be considerable genetic and phenotypic change without the loss of the capacity for interbreeding. When interbreeding is mechanically possible but prevented by the geographical separation of populations, the groups are regarded as subspecies.

The African elephant has been regarded as a single species. It has been recently discovered that there are morphological and DNA differences between elephants in Africa. Some researchers have made the argument that geographic isolation has gone on long enough to create separate species. If accepted, this theory would separate the West African elephants from the savanna elephants on the rest of the continent.

Skill 3.4   History and Origin of Life

a. Explain the theoretical origins of life on Earth

The hypothesis that life developed on Earth from nonliving materials is widely accepted. The transformation from nonliving materials to life had four stages. The first stage was the nonliving (abiotic) synthesis of small monomers such as amino acids and nucleotides. In the second stage, these monomers combined to form polymers, such as proteins and nucleic acids. The third stage was the accumulation of these polymers into droplets called protobionts. The last stage was the origin of heredity, with RNA as the first genetic material.

The first stage of this theory was hypothesized in the 1920s. A. I. Oparin and J. B. S. Haldane were the first to theorize that the primitive atmosphere was a reducing atmosphere with no oxygen present. The gases were rich in hydrogen, methane, water, and ammonia. In the 1950s, Stanley Miller proved Oparin's theory in the laboratory by combining the above gases. When given an electrical spark, he was able to synthesize simple amino acids. It is commonly accepted that amino acids appeared before DNA. Other laboratory experiments have supported that the other stages in the origin of life theory could have happened.

Other scientists believe simpler hereditary systems originated before nucleic acids. In 1991, Julius Rebek was able to synthesize a simple organic molecule that replicates itself. According to his theory, this simple molecule may be the precursor of RNA.

Prokaryotes are the simplest life form. Their small genome size limits the number of genes that control metabolic activities. Over time, some prokaryotic groups became multicellular organisms for this reason. Prokaryotes then evolved to form complex bacterial communities where species benefit from one another.

The **endosymbiotic theory** of the origin of eukaryotes states that eukaryotes arose from symbiotic groups of prokaryotic cells. According to this theory, smaller prokaryotes lived within larger prokaryotic cells, eventually evolving into chloroplasts and mitochondria.

Chloroplasts are the descendant of photosynthetic prokaryotes and mitochondria are likely the descendants of bacteria that were aerobic heterotrophs. Serial endosymbiosis is a sequence of endosymbiotic events. Serial endosymbiosis may also play a role in the progression of life forms to become eukaryotes.

b. Construct a branching diagram (cladogram) from a variety of data sources illustrating the phylogeny between organisms of currently identified taxonomic groups

The typical graphic product of a classification is a **phylogenetic tree**, which represents a hypothesis of the relationships based on branching of lineages within a group through time.

Every time you see a phylogenetic tree, you should be aware that it is making statements on the degree of similarity between organisms, or the particular pattern in which the various lineages diverged (phylogenetic history).

Cladistics is the study of phylogenetic relationships of organisms by analysis of shared, derived character states. Cladograms are constructed to show evolutionary pathways. Character states are polarized in cladistic analysis to be plesiomorphous (ancestral features), symplesiomorphous (shared ancestral features), apomorphous (derived features), and synapomorphous (shared, derived features).

A cladogram is a branching diagram that uses the development of novel traits to separate groups of organisms. While cladograms do not address the relative importance of certain characteristics, they do show when, in relation to others, characteristics developed. In evolution populations are altered over time and may speciate into separate branches, hybridize together, or terminate by extinction. The development (ontogeny) of an organism may give clues about its ancestry (phylogeny).

The starting point for the construction of a cladogram is a table of data displaying the characteristics of each organism. Consider the following table. Plus (+) indicates the presence of a trait and minus (-) indicates the lack of a trait.

	jaws	placenta	hair	opposable thumb	upright posture	multicellular	limbs
Human	+	+	+	+	+	+	+
E. coli	-	-	-	-	-	-	-
Kangaroo	+	-	+	-	-	+	+
Sponge	-	-	-	-	-	+	-
Chimpanzee	+	+	+	+	-	+	+
Tiger	+	+	+	-	-	+	+
Newt	+	-	-	-	-	+	+
Trout	+	-	-	-	-	+	-

To construct the cladogram from the table, we begin with the organism possessing the fewest of the observed traits and branch off each organism as a novel trait appears. In this case, we begin with *E. coli*, possessing none of the observed traits, and end with humans, possessing all of the observed traits.

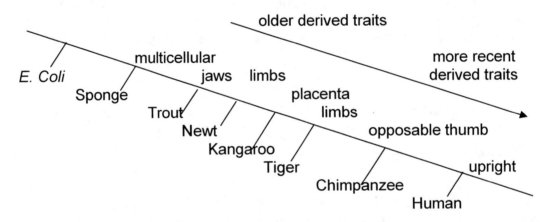

Note the distinguishing trait that creates each branch, listed at the branch points. Note also that the order of the branches reveals the order in which the distinguishing traits derived.

Competency 4.0   Ecology

Skill 4.1   Biodiversity

a. Define biodiversity and describe the effects on biodiversity of alteration of habitat

Biodiversity, or biological diversity, is the diversity of life. One can measure biodiversity by researching how many individuals are present in a species, how many species exist in any ecosystem, how many ecosystems exist in an area, etc. The current species extinction rate is an estimated 100 times greater than the pre-human extinction rate. This rapid loss of biodiversity has potentially grave consequences beyond the typical aesthetic and ethical concerns. Ecological disruption caused by the loss of biodiversity can negatively affect human health and hinder medical treatment and research.

Alteration of habitat disrupts an ecosystem's balance, causing organisms to flee, adapt to a changing environment, or, in a worst case scenario, become extinct. Humans have been infringing upon animal habitats for years by engaging in activities such as logging, commercial fishing, and the building of tourist areas/hotels along waterways/ocean. The long-term effects of this behavior are just beginning to be apparent.

Species of plants, animals, and microorganisms interact to complete many important ecological tasks such as gas exchange, water filtration, soil fertilization, and temperature and precipitation regulation. The loss of only a few species to extinction can disrupt the fine balance that drives these important processes. Even species that are functionally redundant are important because they serve as buffers against environmental change. An environmental change such as a change in climate change may lessen the productivity of one species, but the presence of another species that can fulfill the same ecological function allows the ecosystem to continue without disruption. Disruption of ecosystem function due to loss of biodiversity can negatively affect human health. Increased pollution and decreased soil quality are two human causes of ecosystems becoming disrupted.

A lack of biodiversity can also induce the emergence and spread of infectious disease. Loss of diversity can decrease competition for disease-vector species allowing population growth and increased disease-spreading capability. For example, the extinction of the natural competitors and predators of white footed mice in North American forests led to an increase in the population of this Lyme disease-carrying species. As a result, the incidence of Lyme disease skyrocketed.

Finally, loss of biodiversity can negatively affect human health by eliminating potential medical treatments and hampering medical research. Many pharmaceutical drugs come from natural sources and the premature loss of species eliminates the possibility of new drug discovery. In addition, studying different species helps scientists understand physiology and disease mechanisms. In other words, medical research suffers when species become extinct.

Skill 4.2   Energy Flow and Nutrient Cycles

a. Evaluate the importance of stability of producers, consumers, and decomposers

Trophic levels are based on the feeding relationships that determine energy flow and chemical cycling.

Autotrophs are the primary producers of the ecosystem. **Producers** mainly consist of plants. **Primary consumers** are the next trophic level. The primary consumers are the herbivores that eat plants or algae. **Secondary consumers** are the carnivores that eat the primary consumers. **Tertiary consumers** eat the secondary consumer. These trophic levels may go higher depending on the ecosystem. **Decomposers** are consumers that feed off animal waste and dead organisms. This pathway of food transfer is the food chain.

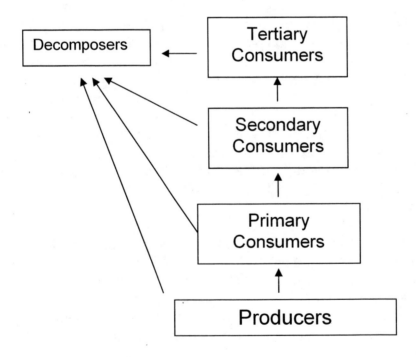

Most food chains are more elaborate, thus becoming food webs.

Energy is lost as the trophic levels progress up the chain from producer to tertiary consumer. The amount of energy that is transferred between trophic levels is called the ecological efficiency. The visual of this energy flow is represented in a **pyramid of productivity**. Producers are at the bottom of the pyramid.

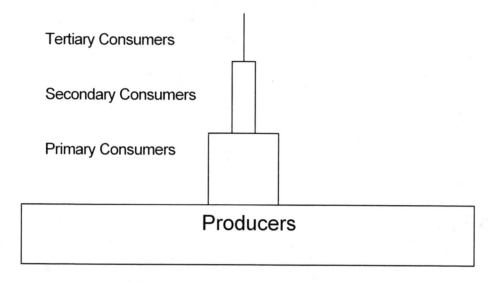

The **biomass pyramid** represents the total dry weight of organisms in each trophic level. A **pyramid of numbers** is a representation of the population size of each trophic level. The producers, being the most populous, are on the bottom of this pyramid with the tertiary consumers on the top with the fewest numbers.

Biogeochemical cycles

Biogeochemical cycles are nutrient cycles that involve both biotic and abiotic factors.

Water cycle - Two percent of all the available water is fixed and unavailable in ice or the bodies of organisms. Available water includes surface water (e.g., lakes, oceans, rivers) and ground water (e.g., aquifers, wells). 96% of all available water is from ground water. The water cycle is driven by solar energy. Water is recycled through the processes of evaporation and precipitation. The water present now is the water that has been here since our atmosphere formed.

Carbon cycle - Ten percent of all available carbon in the air (in the form of carbon dioxide gas) is fixed by photosynthesis. Plants fix carbon in the form of glucose. Animals eat the plants and are able to obtain carbon. When animals release carbon dioxide through respiration, the plants again have a source of carbon for further fixation.

Nitrogen cycle - Eighty percent of the atmosphere is in the form of nitrogen gas. Nitrogen must be fixed and taken out of the gaseous form to be incorporated into an organism. Only a few genera of bacteria have the correct enzymes to break the triple bond between nitrogen atoms in a process called nitrogen fixation. These bacteria live within the roots of legumes (e.g., peas, beans, alfalfa) and add nitrogen to the soil so it may be taken up by the plant. Nitrogen is necessary to make amino acids and the nitrogenous bases of DNA.

Phosphorus cycle - Phosphorus exists as a mineral and is not found in the atmosphere. Fungi and plant roots have a structure called mycorrhizae that are able to fix insoluble phosphates into useable phosphorus. Urine and decayed matter return phosphorus to the earth where it can be fixed in the plant. Phosphorus is needed for the backbone of DNA and for ATP manufacturing.

Role of Decomposers

Decomposers recycle the carbon accumulated in durable organic material that does not immediately proceed to the carbon cycle. Ammonification is the decomposition of organic nitrogen back to ammonia. This process in the nitrogen cycle is carried out by aerobic and anaerobic bacterial and fungal decomposers. Decomposers add phosphorous back to the soil by decomposing the excretion of animals.

Stability and disturbances

Nature replenishes itself continually.

Natural disturbances such as landslides and brushfires are not just destructive. Following the destruction, they allow for a new generation of organisms to inhabit the land. For every indigenous organism there exists a natural predator. These predator/prey relationships allow populations to maintain reproductive balance and to not over-utilize food sources, thus keeping food chains in check. Left alone, nature would always find a way to balance itself. Unfortunately, the largest disturbances nature faces are from humans. For example, humans have introduced non-indigenous species to many areas, upsetting the predator/prey relationships. Our building has caused landslides and disrupted waterfront ecosystems. We have damaged the ozone layer and over-utilized the land entrusted to us.

Human impact

The human population has been growing exponentially for centuries. People are living longer and healthier lives than ever before. Better health care and nutrition practices have helped in the survival of the population.

Human activity affects parts of the nutrient cycles by removing nutrients from one part of the biosphere and adding them to another. This results in nutrient depletion in one area and nutrient excess in another. This affects water systems, crops, wildlife, and humans.

Humans are responsible for the depletion of the ozone layer. This depletion is partially a result of chemicals used for refrigeration and aerosols. The consequences of ozone depletion will be severe. Ozone protects the Earth from the majority of UV radiation. An increase of UV will promote skin cancer and unknown effects on wildlife and plants.

Humans have a tremendous impact on the world's natural resources. The world's natural water supplies are affected by human use. Waterways are major sources for recreation and freight transportation. Oil and wastes from boats and cargo ships pollute the aquatic environment. The aquatic plant and animal life is affected by this contamination.

Deforestation for urban development has resulted in the extinction or relocation of several species of plants and animals. Animals are forced to leave their forest homes or perish among the destruction. The number of plant and animal species that have become extinct due to deforestation is unknown. Scientists have only identified a fraction of the species on Earth. It is known that if the destruction of natural resources continues, there may be no plants or animals successfully reproducing in the wild.

Humans are continuously searching for new places to form communities. This encroachment on the environment leads to the destruction of wildlife communities and their habitat.

Conservationists focus on endangered species, but the primary focus should be on protecting the entire biome. If a biome becomes extinct, the wildlife dies or invades another biome.

Preservations established by the government aim to protect small parts of biomes. While beneficial in the conservation of a few areas, the majority of the environment is still unprotected.

Interrelationships among ecosystems

An ecosystem is the collection of all components and processes that define a portion of the biosphere. Ecosystems include both biotic (living) and abiotic (non-living) components. Biotic factors are the living things in the ecosystems like plants, animals, bacteria, and fungi. If just one of these increases in a community, there will be a strain on the available amount of food, water, shelter, and space for the other organisms. The Abiotic facts are the non-living aspects of the ecosystem such as soil quality, rainfall, and temperature. If a new species is introduced to an established ecosystem, there may be limited food water, or shelter. While the behavior of individual organisms in an ecosystem affects other members of the ecosystem, ecosystems themselves are also interrelated. Because the boundaries of ecosystems are not fixed, organisms and other ecosystem products and components can move freely between ecosystems. For example, the waste products from a terrestrial ecosystem may enter an aquatic ecosystem, changing the environmental characteristics. In addition, any ecosystem process that alters the global environment affects all other ecosystems. For example, there are those who produce greenhouse gases that deplete the ozone layer while they fuss about the ways in which global warming affects the global climateand alters the characteristics of ecosystems across the globe.

Skill 4.3   Interrelationships and Change in Ecosystems

a. Describe various species interactions (e.g., predator/prey, parasitism, mutualism, commensalism, competition)

There are many interactions that may occur between different species living together. Predation, parasitism, competition, commensalisms, and mutualism are the different types of relationships individuals in a population have with each other.

Predation and **parasitism** result in a benefit for one species and a detriment for the other. Predation is when on animal (a predator) eats another animal (its prey). The common conception of predation is of a carnivore consuming other animals. This is one form of predation. Although not always resulting in the death of the plant, herbivorism is a form of predation. Some animals eat enough of a plant to cause death. Parasitism involves a predator that lives on or in its host, causing detrimental effects to the host. Insects and viruses living off and reproducing in their hosts is an example of parasitism. Many plants and animals have defenses against predators. Some plants have poisonous chemicals that will harm the predator if ingested and some animals are camouflaged so they are harder to detect.

Competition is when two or more species in a community use the same resources. Competition is usually detrimental to both populations. Competition is often difficult to find in nature because competition between two populations is not continuous. Either the weaker population will cease to exist, or one population will evolve to utilize other available resources.

Symbiosis is when two species live close together. Parasitism is one example of symbiosis described above. Another example of symbiosis is commensalism. **Commensalism** occurs when two species occupy a similar space and one species may benefit from the other, but there are no harmful effects to either. **Mutualism** is when both species occupy a similar space and both benefit from the other. Species involved in mutualistic relationships must coevolve to survive. As one species evolves, the other must also evolve if it is to be successful in life. The grouper fish and a species of shrimp live in a mutualistic relationship. The shrimp feed off of parasites that live on the grouper. Thus, the shrimp are fed and the grouper stays healthy. Many microorganisms exist in mutualistic relationships.

b. Analyze the fluctuations in population size in an ecosystem due to the relative rates of birth, immigration, emigration, and death

Population density is the number of individuals per unit area or volume. The spacing pattern of individuals in an area is dispersion. **Dispersion patterns** can be clumped, with individuals grouped in patches; uniform, where individuals are approximately equidistant from each other; or random.

Population densities are usually estimated based on a few representative plots. Aggregation of a population in a relatively small geographic area can have detrimental effects to the environment. Food, water, and other resources will be rapidly consumed, resulting in an unstable environment. A low population density is less harmful to the environment. The use of natural resources will be more widespread, allowing for the environment to recover and continue growth.

Population density changes to reflect the rates of birth, immigration, emigration, and death. When birth rates are high, population density increases. Conversely, when death rates are high, density decreases, and when birth and death rates are even, the population has reached equilibrium. The same system is true for immigration and emigration. Immigration (organisms coming into the population) swells population density, emigration (organisms leaving the community) decreases it, and when the two are balanced the population is level. More consumers in any one area utilize resources, so it stands to reason that birth and immigration both drain supply, whereas emigration and death decrease the population and its density, thus allowing natural resources to replenish themselves.

c. Analyze changes in an ecosystem resulting from changes in climate, human activity, introduction of nonnative species, and changes in population size

Ecosystems are vulnerable to effects from changes in the climate, human activity, introduction of nonnative species, and changes in population size. Changes in climate can alter the ability of certain organisms to grow. For example, during drought conditions, plants that are less succulent are unable to maintain water regulation and perish. Organisms that previously fed on that particular plant must find a new food source, or they too will perish. When one organism/colony dies, its space is made available for another. For example, after a brush fire, low lying shrubs are the first to die off. Taller, well-established trees with tough bark are most likely to survive a forest fire. In addition, once the ground cools, new plants will emerge; some identical to the previous, but some new-to-the-area plants may intrude as there is a large, open surface area for new species to take root. It is in situations like these that ecosystems are especially vulnerable to the introduction of nonnative species.

The introduction of a nonnative species can effectively wipe out an existing, or indigenous, species. Invasive species are problematic because they reproduce rapidly, spread over large areas, and have few/no natural controls, such as diseases or predators, to keep them in check. Human beings are to blame for the introduction of many nonnative species. For example, Zebra muscles and three different species of rats have all arrived in America as stowaways on ships. Zebra muscles are now established in all the Great Lakes, most of the large, navigable rivers of the eastern United States, and in many lakes in the Great Lakes region. The presence of mussels in the Great Lakes and Hudson River has reduced the biomass of phytoplankton significantly since their accidental introduction in 1980. These nonnative muscles are consuming the phytoplankton on which native species previously fed, and the nonnative species are reproducing faster than the native species. Therefore, not only are native muscles affected, but the local food web is affected by a decrease in its lower level food supply.

As populations increase in size they naturally consume more resources and excrete more waste. These behaviors are a drain to an ecosystem. Sometimes an ecosystem can recover from these changes, but sometimes the damage is too severe. This has never been more true than with the human species. Humans are continuously searching for new places to form communities. This encroachment on the environment leads to the destruction of wildlife communities. Conservationists focus on endangered species, but the primary focus should be on protecting the entire biome. If a biome becomes extinct, the wildlife dies or invades another biome. Preservations established by the government aim at protecting small parts of biomes. While beneficial in the conservation of a few areas, the majority of the environment is still unprotected.

DOMAIN II – Subject Matter Skills and Abilities

Competency 5.0   Investigation and Experimentation

Skill 5.1   Question Formulation

The first step in scientific inquiry is posing a question. Next, a hypothesis is formed to provide a plausible explanation. An experiment is then proposed and performed to test this hypothesis. A comparison between the predicted and observed results is the next step. Conclusions are then formed. The student or scientist must determine whether the hypothesis is correct or incorrect. If incorrect, the next step is to form a new hypothesis and repeat the process.

Let's use the following everyday situation as an example. While making breakfast, you bring three eggs from the refrigerator to the stove. Your hands are full and you accidentally drop an egg on the floor, which immediately shatters. As you clean up the mess you wonder if you had carried the eggs in their cardboard container, would they have broken if dropped? Similarly, if dropped would they have broken on a softer surface, for example linoleum?

a. Formulate and evaluate a viable hypothesis

Once the question is formulated take an educated guess about the answer to the problem or question. For our scientist above, a plausible hypothesis might be that even if dropped, the egg would not have broken if it had been enclosed in its protective cardboard box.

b. Recognize the value and role of observation prior to question formulation

The scientist conducting our imaginary egg experiment made observations prior to the experiment. He knows that eggshells are fragile, and that their interior is liquid. He also noted that his floor was made of tile, a hard surface, and that the broken egg had not been protected. His observations, however general they may have seemed, led him to create a viable question and an educated guess (hypothesis) about what he expected. While scientists often have laboratories set up to study a specific event, it is likely that along the way they will find an unexpected result. It is always important to be open-minded and to look at all of the information. An open-minded approach to science provides room for more questioning, and, hence, more learning.

c. Recognize the iterative nature of questioning

The questioning stage of scientific inquiry involves repetition. By repeating the experiment you can discover whether or not you have reproducibility.

If results are reproducible, the hypothesis is valid. If the results are not reproducible, one has more questions to ask.

d. Given an experimental design, identify possible hypotheses that it may test

An experiment is proposed and performed with the sole objective of testing a hypothesis. You discover the aforementioned scientist conducting an experiment with the following characteristics. He has two rows, each set up with four stations. The first row has a piece of tile as the base at each station. The second row has a piece of linoleum as the base at each station. The scientist has eight eggs and is prepared to drop one over each station. What is he testing? He is trying to answer whether or not the egg is more likely to break when dropped on one material as opposed to the other. His hypothesis might have been: The egg will be less likely to break when dropped on linoleum.

Skill 5.2   Planning a Scientific Investigation (including Experimental Design)

a. Given a hypothesis, formulate an investigation or experimental design to test that hypothesis

Suppose our junior scientist wants address his initial question, "if you had carried the eggs in their cardboard container, would they have broken if dropped?" A sensible hypothesis to this question would be that an egg would be less likely to break if it was dropped in its cardboard container, than if it were unprotected. Because reproducibility is important, we need to set up multiple identical stations, or use the same station for repeatedly conducting the same experiment. Either way it is key that everything is identical. If the scientist wants to study the break rate for one egg in it's container, then it needs to be just one egg dropped each time in an identical way. The investigator should systematically walk to each station and drop an egg over each station and record the results. The first four times, the egg should be dropped without enclosing it in a cardboard carton. This is the control. It is a recreation of what happened accidentally in the kitchen and one would expect the results to be the same; an egg dropped onto tile will break. The next four times, the egg should be dropped nestled within its original, store-manufactured, cardboard container. One would expect that the egg would not break, or would break less often under these conditions.

b. Evaluate an experimental design for its suitability to test a given hypothesis

When designing an experiment, one needs to clearly define what one is testing. One also needs to consider the question asked. The more limited the question, the easier it is to set up an experiment to answer it.

Theoretically, if an egg were dropped, the egg would be safest when dropped in a protective carton over a soft surface. However, one should not measure multiple variables at once. Studying multiple variables at once makes the results difficult to analyze. How would the investigator discern which variable was responsible for the result? When evaluating experimental design, make sure to look at the number of variables, how clearly they were defined, and how accurately they were measured. Also consider if the experiment was applicable. Did it make sense and address the hypothesis?

c. Distinguish between variable and controlled parameters

The procedure used to obtain data is important to the outcome. Experiments consist of **controls** and **variables**. A control is the experiment run under normal, unmanipulated conditions.

A variable is a factor or condition the scientist manipulates. In biology, the variable may be light, temperature, pH, time, etc. Scientists can use the differences in tested variables to make predictions or test hypotheses. Only one variable should be tested at a time. In other words, one would not alter both the temperature and pH of the experimental subject.

An **independent variable** is one the researcher directly changes or manipulates. This could be the amount of light given to a plant or the temperature at which bacteria is grown. The **dependent variable** is the factor that changes due to the influence of the independent variable. In measuring the effects of different quantities of fertilizer on plant growth, the independent variable would be the amount of fertilizer used on each plant. The dependent variables would be height, number of leaves, amount or size of fruit, or even the mass of the plant. The researcher would use identical plants in identical pots each with the same amount of the same soil and place all plants so that they receive the same amount of light and water. These would be the controls. Because these are controlled, the plants would have different rates of growth as a direct result of the different amounts of fertilizer.

Skill 5.3   Observation and Data Collection

a. Identify changes in natural phenomena over time without manipulating the phenomena (e.g. a tree limb, a grove of trees, a stream, a hill slope).

Scientists identify changes in natural phenomena over time using basic tools of measurement and observation. Scientists measure growth of plants by measuring plant dimensions at different time intervals, changes in plant and animal populations by counting, and changes in environmental conditions by observation. The following are four examples of natural phenomena and the observation techniques used to measure change in each case.

To identify change in a tree limb, we measure the dimensions (length, circumference) of the limb at different time intervals. In addition, we can study the types and amount of organisms growing on the limb by observing a small sample and applying the observations to make estimations about the entire limb. Finally, we can watch for the presence of disease or bacterial infection by observing the color and consistency of the limb and any changes over time.

To identify change in a grove of trees, we employ similar techniques as used in the observation of a tree limb. First, we count the number of each type of tree in the grove. Then we measure the size of the trees at different time intervals.

If the grove contains many trees, we may measure only a representative sample of trees and apply the results to make conjectures about the grove population. Finally, we closely monitor the trees for changes that may indicate disease or infection.

To identify change in a stream, we measure and observe characteristics of both the stream itself and the organisms living in it. First, we measure the width and depth of the stream at different time intervals to monitor erosion. Second, we observe the water level at different time intervals to monitor the effect of weather patterns. Finally, using sampling techniques, we observe and measure the types and number of organisms present in the stream and how these characteristics change over time.

To identify change on a hill slope, we measure the angle and dimensions of the slope at different time intervals to monitor the effects of erosion by wind and rain. In addition, we use sampling techniques to make generalizations about the organisms living on the slope. We might take soil samples at various places on the hill to determine the types of soil and the depths of each type in each place. We would repeat that at different time intervals to monitor changes. Finally, we can monitor how the types and amounts of vegetation on the slope change in relation to the change in the angle of the slope (i.e. determine which types of plants have the ability to grow in certain conditions).

b. Analyze the locations, sequences, and time intervals that are characteristic of natural phenomena (e.g. locations of planets over time, succession of species in an ecosystem).

One of the main goals of science is the study and explanation of natural phenomena. When studying natural phenomena, scientists describe the characteristic locations, sequences, and time intervals. Examples of natural phenomena studied by scientists include the locations of planets over time and the succession of species in an ecosystem.

The eight planets of the solar system (Pluto was formerly included as a planet but has been removed as of Summer 2006) orbit the sun in a specific sequence. The time it takes to complete an orbit of the Sun is different for each planet. In addition, we can determine the location of each planet in relation to the Sun and to each other using mathematical models and charts.

Mercury orbits closest to the sun, followed by Venus, Earth, Mars, Jupiter, Saturn, Uranus, and Neptune. Neptune is farthest from the Sun for 20 of every 248 years. Planets will never collide because one is always higher than the other, even when their orbits do intersect.

The amount of time a planet takes to complete one orbit of the Sun increases as the distance from the Sun increases. This value, called the sidereal period, ranges from 0.241 years for Mercury to 248.1 years for Neptune.

The synodic period measures the amount of time it takes for a planet to return to the same point in the sky as observed from Earth. Mercury has the shortest synodic period of 116 days while Mars has the longest of 780 days. The synodic periods of Jupiter, Saturn, Uranus, and Neptune are similar, slightly less than 400 days for each.

Succession of species is the change in the type and number of plants, animals, and microorganisms that occurs periodically in all ecosystems. The two types of succession are primary and secondary. Primary succession describes the creation and subsequent development of a new, unoccupied habitat (e.g. a lava flow). Secondary succession describes the disruption of an existing community (e.g. fire, human tampering, and flood) and the response of the community to the disruption. Succession is usually a very long process. New communities often take hundreds or thousands of years to reach a fully developed state (climax community). And, while succession in climax communities is minimal, environmental disruption can easily restart the succession process.

In general, simple organisms (e.g. bacteria, small plants) dominate new communities and prepare the environment for the development of larger, more complex species. For example, the dominant vegetation of an empty field will progress sequentially from grasses to small shrubs to soft wood trees to hard wood trees. We can observe and measure succession in two ways. First, we can measure the changes in a single community over time. Second, we can observe and compare similar communities at different stages of development. We are limited in the amount of data we can gather using the first method because of the slow nature of the succession process. The techniques used to observe succession include fossil observation, geological study, and environmental sampling.

c. Select and use appropriate tools and technology (e.g. computer-linked probes, spreadsheets, graphing calculators) to perform tests, collect data, analyze relationships, and display data.

Biologists use a variety of tools and technologies to perform tests, collect and display data, and analyze relationships. Examples of commonly used tools include computer-linked probes, spreadsheets, and graphing calculators.

Biologists use computer-linked probes to measure various environmental factors including temperature, dissolved oxygen, pH, ionic concentration, and pressure. The advantage of computer-linked probes, as compared to more traditional observational tools, is that the probes automatically gather data and present it in an accessible format. This property of computer-linked probes eliminates the need for constant human observation and manipulation which, in turn, eliminates the possibility of human errors.

Biologists use spreadsheets to organize, analyze, and display data. For example, conservation ecologists use spreadsheets to model population growth and development, apply sampling techniques, and create statistical distributions to analyze relationships. Spreadsheet use simplifies data collection and manipulation and allows the presentation of data in a logical and understandable format.

Graphing calculators are another technology with many applications to biology. For example, biologists use algebraic functions to analyze growth, development, and other natural processes. Graphing calculators can manipulate algebraic data and create graphs for analysis and observation. In addition, biologists use the matrix function of graphing calculators to model problems in genetics. The use of graphing calculators simplifies the creation of graphical displays including histograms, scatter plots, and line graphs. Biologists can also transfer data and displays to computers for further analysis. Finally, biologists connect computer-linked probes, used to collect data, to graphing calculators to ease the collection, transmission, and analysis of data.

d. Evaluate the precision, accuracy, and reproducibility of data

Accuracy is the degree of conformity of a measured, calculated quantity to its actual (true) value. Precision, also called reproducibility or repeatability, is the degree to which further measurements or calculations will show the same or similar results.

Accuracy is the degree of veracity while precision is the degree of reproducibility. The best analogy to explain accuracy and precision is the target comparison. Repeated measurements are compared to arrows that are fired at a target. Accuracy describes the closeness of arrows to the bull's eye at the target center. Arrows that strike closer to the bull's eye are considered more accurate. Precision, on the other hand, describes a cluster of arrows that land in the same location, distant from the target bull's eye.

e. Identify and analyze possible reasons for inconsistent results, such as sources of error or uncontrolled conditions

Reproducibility is highly important in science. If results are not reproducible, they are usually not given much credit, regardless of the hypothesis. For this reason, we pay close attention to minimizing sources of error. Examples of common sources of error might be contamination or an improperly mixed buffer. In addition, one should remember that scientists are humans, and human error is always a possibility.

All experimental uncertainty is due to either random error or systematic error.

Random errors usually result from the experimenter's inability to take the same measurement in exactly the same way to get exactly the same number. Random errors can result from limitations in equipment or techniques. A random error decreases precision. All measurements should be reported to a proper number of significant digits that include an imprecise final digit to reflect random error.

Systematic errors, on the other hand, are reproducible inaccuracies that are consistently in the same direction. Systematic errors are often due to a problem that persists throughout the entire experiment such as imperfect equipment or technique. Systematic error decreases accuracy. Instead of a random error with random fluctuations, there is a biased result. Systematic and random errors refer to problems associated with making measurements. Mistakes made in the calculations or in reading the instrument are not considered in error analysis.

f. Identify and communicate sources of unavoidable experimental error

Unavoidable experimental error is the random error inherent in scientific experiments regardless of the methods used. One source of unavoidable error is measurement and the use of measurement devices. Using measurement devices is an imprecise process because it is often impossible to accurately read measurements. For example, when using a ruler to measure the length of an object, if the length falls between markings on the ruler, we must estimate the true value. Another source of unavoidable error is the randomness of population sampling and the behavior of any random variable. For example, when sampling a population we cannot guarantee that our sample is completely representative of the larger population. In addition, because we cannot constantly monitor the behavior of a random variable, any observations necessarily contain some level of unavoidable error.

g. Recognize the issues of statistical variability and explain the need for controlled tests

Statistical variability is the deviation of an individual in a population from the mean of the population. Variability is inherent in biology because living things are innately unique. For example, the individual weights of humans vary greatly from the mean weight of the population. Thus, when conducting experiments involving the study of living things, we must control for innate variability. Control groups are identical to the experimental group in every way with the exception of the variable being studied. Comparing the experimental group to the control group allows us to determine the effects of the manipulated variable in relation to statistical variability.

h. Know and evaluate the safety issues when designing an experiment and implement appropriate solutions to safety problems

All science labs should contain the following **safety equipment**.:

-Fire blanket that is visible and accessible.
-Ground Fault Circuit Interrupters (GFCI) within two feet of water supplies
-Signs designating room exits.
-Emergency shower providing a continuous flow of water.
-Emergency eye wash station that can be activated by the foot or forearm.
-Eye protection for every student.
-A means of sanitizing equipment.
-Emergency exhaust fans providing ventilation to the outside of the building.
-Master cut-off switches for gas, electric, and compressed air. Switches must have permanently attached handles. Cut-off switches must be clearly labeled.
-An ABC fire extinguisher.
-Storage cabinets for flammable materials.
-Chemical spill control kit.

-Fume hood with a motor that is spark proof.
-Protective laboratory aprons made of flame retardant material.
-Signs that will alert of potential hazardous conditions.
-Labeled containers for broken glassware, flammables, corrosives, and waste.

Students should wear safety goggles when performing dissections, heating, or while using acids and bases. Hair should always be tied back and objects should never be placed in the mouth. Food should not be consumed while in the laboratory. Hands should always be washed before and after laboratory experiments. In case of an accident, eye washes and showers should be used for eye contamination or a chemical spill that covers the student's body. Small chemical spills should only be contained and cleaned by the teacher.

Kitty litter or a chemical spill kit should be used to clean a spill. For large spills, the school administration and the local fire department should be notified. Biological spills should only be handled by the teacher. Contamination with biological waste can be cleaned by using bleach when appropriate. Accidents and injuries should always be reported to the school administration and local health facilities. The severity of the accident or injury will determine the course of action.

It is the responsibility of the teacher to provide a safe environment for his or her students. Proper supervision greatly reduces the risk of injury and a teacher should never leave a class for any reason without providing alternate supervision. After an accident, two factors are considered, **foreseeability** and **negligence**. Foreseeability is the anticipation that an event may occur under certain circumstances. Negligence is the failure to exercise ordinary or reasonable care. Safety procedures should be a part of the science curriculum and a well managed classroom is important to avoid potential lawsuits.

Teachers should observe student behavior closely, which is very important in a science class where experiments are sometimes done using chemicals, live animals, etc. In these situations, students need to behave properly since their own safety and that of others are involved. It is important that the students be observed very carefully and any unwanted and inappropriate behavior be corrected immediately.

In designing experiments, it is important to:

- Use the smallest amount of chemical needed at the lowest concentration for the shortest time period possible.
- When feasible, substitute less hazardous chemicals for chemicals with greater hazards in experiments.
- Assess hazards, worst case scenarios, and potential risks prior to starting the experiment and have a written plan for dealing with each.
- Be careful when using animals in experiments that all procedures are humane and animals receive good care (including appropriate food and water) throughout the experiment.

i. Appropriately employ a variety of print and electronic resources (e.g. the World Wide Web) to collect information and evidence as part of a research project

Scientists use print and electronic resources to collect information and evidence. Gathering information from scientific literature is a necessary element in successful research project design. Scientific journals, a major source of scientific information, provide starting points for experimental design and points of comparison in the interpretation of experimental results. Examples of important scientific journals are *Science*, *Nature*, and *Cell*. Scientists use the World Wide Web to search and access scientific journal articles through databases such as PubMed, JSTOR, and Google Scholar. In addition, the World Wide Web is a rich source of basic background information useful in the design and implementation of research projects. Examples of relevant online resources include scientific encyclopedias, general science websites, and research laboratory homepages. Many colleges post class notes, lab procedures, and other pertinent information on the World Wide Web so that it can often be found using a Google or Yahoo search.

j. Assess the accuracy validity and reliability of information gathered from a variety of sources

Because people often attempt to use scientific evidence in support of political or personal agendas, the ability to evaluate the credibility of scientific claims is a necessary skill in today's society. In evaluating scientific claims made in the media, public debates, and advertising, one should follow several guidelines.

First, scientific, peer-reviewed journals are the most accepted source for information on scientific experiments and studies. One should carefully scrutinize any claim that does not reference peer-reviewed literature.

Second, the media and those with an agenda to advance (e.g., advertisers and debaters) often overemphasize the certainty and importance of experimental results. One should question any scientific claim that sounds either too good to be true or overly certain.

Finally, knowledge of experimental design and the scientific method is important in evaluating the credibility of studies. For example, one should look for the inclusion of control groups and the presence of data to support the given conclusions. Other things to observe before validating the experiment include length of time for the experiment, number of subjects, repeatability of the experiment, how many variables were tested and how they were tested, and whether the conclusions match the evidence.

Skill 5.4   Data Analysis/Graphing

a. Construct appropriate graphs from data and develop qualitative and quantitative statements about relationships between variables

Graphing is an important technique for the visual display of collected data for analysis. The two types of graphs most commonly used are the **line graph** and the **bar graph** (histogram).

The type of graphic representation used to display observations depends on the type of data collected. **Scatter plots** show possible relationships between two variables. They are used to help the experimenter to decide if some partial or indirect relationship – a correlation – exists. **Line graphs** compare different sets of related data and help predict data. For example, a line graph could compare the rate of activity of different enzymes at varying temperatures. A **bar graph** or **histogram** compares different items and helps make comparisons based on the data. For example, a bar graph could compare the ages of children in a classroom. A **pie chart** is useful when organizing data as part of a whole. For example, a pie chart could display the percent of time students spend on various after school activities.

A scatter plot is the simplest type of graph. It simply plots the data points against their values, without adding any connecting lines, bars, or other features. The first variable is measured along the x-axis and the second along the y-axis.

Line graphs show two variables represented by one point on the graph. Line graphs are useful when the data points are more important than the transitions between them. They are best at showing a long series of data points, general trends, or changes over time. The X-axis is the horizontal axis and represents the dependent variable. Dependent variables are those that are present independent of the experiment. A common example of a dependent variable is time. Time proceeds regardless of anything else going on. The Y-axis is the vertical axis and represents the independent variable. Independent variables are the factor that is manipulated in the experiment. An example of an independent variable is the amount of light received by a plant .

Graphs should be calibrated at equal intervals. If one space represents one day, the next space may not represent ten days. A "best fit" line is drawn to join the points and may not include all the points in the data. Different series of points are shown by giving them different line markings – for example, dashed or dotted – or different tick marks. Axes must always be labeled. A good title will describe both the dependent and the independent variable.

Bar graphs are set up similarly in regards to axes, but points are not plotted. Instead, the dependent variable is set up as a bar where the X-axis intersects with the Y-axis. Each bar is a separate item of data and is not joined by a continuous line. Bar graphs are good for looking at differences amongst similar things. If the data are a time series, a carefully chosen column graph is generally more appropriate but bar graphs can be used to vary a presentation when many column graphs of time series are used. One advantage of bar graphs is that there is greater horizontal space for variable descriptors because the vertical axis is the category axis.

A pie chart is a circle with radii connecting the center to the edge. The area between two radii is called a slice. Data values are proportionate to the angle between the radii. Pie charts best show parts of a whole. Six slices are typically as many as can be handled on one pie.

When drawing conclusions from graphs, one can make quantitative or qualitative statements. Quantitative is derived from quantity (numerical, precise) and qualitative (impressive such as a trend) is derived from quality. For example, stating that the median is 12 would be a quantitative assessment.

b. Recognize the slope of the linear graph as the constant in the relationship y=kx and apply this principle in interpreting graphs constructed from data

Analyzing graphs is a useful method for determining the mathematical relationship between the dependent and independent variables of an experiment. The usefulness of the method lies in the fact that the variables on the axes of a straight-line graph are represented by the expression, $y = m*x + b$, where m is the slope of the line and b is the y-intercept of the line. This equation works only if the data fit a straight-line graph. Thus, once the data set has been collected, modified, and plotted to achieve a straight-line graph, we can derive the mathematical equation.

c. Apply simple mathematical relationships to determine a missing quantity in an algebraic expression, given the two remaining terms (e.g., speed = distance/time, density = mass/volume, force = pressure x area, volume = area x height)

Science and mathematics are related. Scientific data is strongest and most relevant when accurate, and is, therefore, described in terms of units. To acquire proper units, one must apply appropriate math skills. Some common examples include speed, density, force, and volume. Let us look at density –

$D = m/v$
Where
D = density g/cm^3
m = mass in grams
v = volume in cm^3

We substitute known quantities for the alphabetical symbols. It is absolutely important to write the appropriate units [e.g., g (gram), cm^3 (cubic centimeter)]. This is fundamental algebra.

Thus,

$D = m/v$ becomes g/cm^3 = g divided by cm^3

The second example is the formula for calculating momentum of an object.

Momentum (kg-m/s) = mass (kg) times velocity (meters/second)
$M = mv$
The units of momentum are kg-m/s

d. Determine whether a relationship on a given graph is linear or non-linear and determine the appropriateness of extrapolating the data

The individual data points on the graph of a linear relationship cluster around a line of best fit. In other words, a relationship is linear if we can sketch a straight line that roughly fits the data points. There should be about the same number of points above the line as there are below the line. Consider the following examples of linear and non-linear relationships.

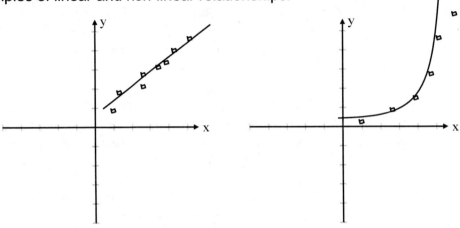

Linear Relationship   Non-Linear Relationship

Note that the non-linear relationship, an exponential relationship in this case, appears linear in parts of the curve. In addition, contrast the preceding graphs to the graph of a data set that shows no relationship between variables.

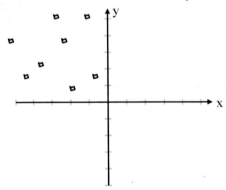

Extrapolation is the process of estimating data points outside a known set of data points. When extrapolating data of a linear relationship, we extend the line of best fit beyond the known values. The extension of the line represents the estimated data points. Extrapolating data is only appropriate if we are relatively certain that the relationship is indeed linear. For example, the death rate of an emerging disease may increase rapidly at first and level off as time goes on. Thus, extrapolating the death rate as if it were linear would yield inappropriately high values at later times.

Similarly, extrapolating certain data in a strictly linear fashion, with no restrictions, may yield obviously inappropriate results. For instance, if the number of plant species in a forest were decreasing with time in a linear fashion, extrapolating the data set to infinity would eventually yield a negative number of species, which is clearly unreasonable.

e. Solve scientific problems by using quadratic equations and simple trigonometric, exponential, and logarithmic functions

Scientists use mathematical tools and equations to model and solve scientific problems. Solving scientific problems often involves the use of quadratic, trigonometric, exponential, and logarithmic functions.

Quadratic equations take the standard form $ax^2 + bx + c = 0$. The most appropriate method of solving quadratic equations in scientific problems is the use of the quadratic formula. The quadratic formula produces the solutions of a standard form quadratic equation.

$$x = \frac{-b \pm \sqrt{b^2 - 4ac}}{2a}$$ {Quadratic Formula}

One common application of quadratic equations is the description of biochemical reaction equilibriums. Consider the following problem.

Example 1

80.0 g of ethanoic acid (MW = 60g) reacts with 85.0 g of ethanol (MW = 46g) until equilibrium. The equilibrium constant is 4.00. Determine the amounts of ethyl acetate and water produced at equilibrium.

$CH_3COOH + CH_3CH_2OH = CH_3CO_2C_2H_5 + H_2O$

The equilibrium constant, K, describes equilibrium of the reaction, relating the concentrations of products to reactants.

$$K = \frac{[CH_3CO_2C_2H_5][H_2O]}{[CH_3CO_2H][CH_3CH_2OH]} = 4.00$$

The equilibrium values of reactants and products are listed in the following table.

	CH_3COOH	CH_3CH_2OH	$CH_3CO_2C_2H_5$	H_2O
Initial	80/60 = 1.33 mol	85/46 = 1.85 mol	0	0
Equilibrium	1.33 − x	1.85 − x	x	x

Thus, K = $\dfrac{[x][x]}{[1.33-x][1.85-x]} = \dfrac{x^2}{2.46-3.18x+x^2} = 4.00$.

Rearrange the equation to produce a standard form quadratic equation.

$$\frac{x^2}{2.46-3.18x+x^2} = 4.00$$

$$x^2 = 4.00(2.46-3.18x+x^2) = 9.84-12.72x+4x^2$$

$$0 = 3x^2 - 12.72x + 9.84$$

Use the quadratic formula to solve for x.

$$x = \frac{-(-12.72)\pm\sqrt{(-12.72)^2 - 4(3)(9.84)}}{2(3)} = 3.22 \text{ or } 1.02$$

3.22 is not an appropriate answer, because we started with only 3.18 moles of reactants. Thus, the amount of each product produced at equilibrium is 1.02 moles.

Scientists use trigonometric functions to define angles and lengths. For example, field biologists can use trigonometric functions to estimate distances and directions. The basic trigonometric functions are sine, cosine, and tangent. Consider the following triangle describing these relationships.

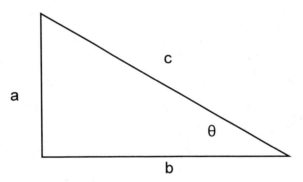

$$\sin\theta = \frac{a}{c}, \cos\theta = \frac{b}{c}, \tan\theta = \frac{a}{b}$$

Exponential functions are useful in modeling many scientific phenomena. For example, scientists use exponential functions to describe bacterial growth and radioactive decay. The general form of exponential equations is $f(x) = Ca^x$ (C is a constant). Consider the following problem involving bacterial growth.

Example 2

Determine the number of bacteria present in a culture inoculated with a single bacterium after 24 hours if the bacterial population doubles every 2 hours. Use $N(t) = N_0 e^{kt}$ as a model of bacterial growth where N(t) is the size of the population at time t, N_0 is the initial population size, and k is the growth constant.

We must first determine the growth constant, k. At t = 2, the size of the population doubles from 1 to 2. Thus, we substitute and solve for k.

$2 = 1(e^{2k})$

$\ln 2 = \ln e^{2k}$ Take the natural log of each side.

$\ln 2 = 2k(\ln e) = 2k$ $\ln e = 1$

$k = \dfrac{\ln 2}{2}$ Solve for k.

The population size at t = 24 is

$N(24) = e^{(\frac{\ln 2}{2})24} = e^{12\ln 2} = 4096$.

Finally, logarithmic functions have many applications to science and biology. One simple example of a logarithmic application is the pH scale. Scientists define pH as follows.

pH = - $\log_{10}$ [H+], where [H+] is the concentration of hydrogen ions

Thus, we can determine the pH of a solution with a [H+] value of 0.0005 mol/L by using the logarithmic formula.

pH = - $\log_{10}$ [0.0005] = 3.3

Skill 5.5   Drawing Conclusions and Communicating Explanations

The state of California needs to ensure that its licensed teachers are capable of performing all the tasks in the list below. These items are not items that can be explained in essay format; rather they are an accumulation of years of learning. You will be able to find correlations with these items in other areas of this manual.

a. Draw appropriate and logical conclusions from data
b. Communicate the logical connection among hypotheses, science concepts, tests conducted, data collected, and conclusions drawn from the scientific evidence
c. Communicate the steps and results of an investigation in written reports and oral presentations
d. Recognize whether evidence is consistent with a proposed explanation
e. Construct appropriate visual representations of scientific phenomena and processes (e.g., motion of Earth's plates, cell structure)
f. Read topographic and geologic maps for evidence provided on the maps and construct and interpret a simple scale map

Competency 6.0   Nature of Science

Skill 6.1   Scientific Inquiry

a. Distinguish among the terms hypothesis, theory, and prediction as used in scientific investigations

Science is a body of knowledge systematically derived from study, observations, and experimentation. Its goal is to identify and establish principles and theories that may be applied to solve problems. Pseudoscience, on the other hand, is a body of beliefs that are not supported by hard evidence. In other words, there is no scientific methodology or application. Some classic examples of pseudoscience include witchcraft, alien encounters, or any topic explained by hearsay.

Scientific experimentation must be repeatable. Experimentation results in theories that can be disproved and changed. Science depends on communication, agreement, and disagreement among scientists. It is composed of theories, laws, and hypotheses.

Theory - A statement of principles or relationships relating to a natural event or phenomenon, which have been verified and accepted.

Law - An explanation of events that occur with uniformity under the same conditions (e.g., laws of nature, law of gravitation).

Hypothesis - An unproved theory or educated guess followed by research to best explain a phenomena. A theory is a proven hypothesis.

Science is limited by the available technology. An example of this would be the relationship between the discovery of the cell and the invention of the microscope. As our technology improves, more hypotheses will become theories and possibly laws. Data collection methods also limit scientific inquiry. Data may be interpreted differently on different occasions. Limitations of scientific methodology produce explanations that change as new technologies emerge.

The first step in scientific inquiry is posing a question. Next, a hypothesis is formed to provide a plausible explanation. An experiment is then proposed, the steps are drawn up, and the experiment is performed to test this hypothesis. A comparison between the predicted and observed results is the next step. Conclusions are then formed and it is determined whether the hypothesis is correct or incorrect. If incorrect, the next step is to form a new hypothesis and repeat the process.

b. Evaluate the usefulness, limitations, and interdisciplinary and cumulative nature of scientific evidence as it relates to the development of models and theories as representations of reality

Presenters of data can manipulate any evidence to serve their own purposes. This is why it is important to carefully evaluate resources. For instance, when reading a scientific article you should ask the following questions. Is it published in a well known journal? Does it use controls? Does it make sense? Is the experiment clearly explained? Are the results reproducible?

One must also recognize the limitations of research. An experiment is easier to analyze if it only has one variable. Would the research still be true if another variable, for example, heat, time, or substrate were changed? One must consider the conditions under which the research was conducted. Were the most advanced technological machines used, or would there be a more applicable way to study the issue? For example, no one realized there was more to know about microscopic life until microscopy became more advanced. We now use scanning electron microscopes (SEM's), making light microscopes somewhat obsolete, and opening our eyes to a whole new level of thoroughness.

As technology changes, so too does our knowledge and our awareness of reality. Galileo was a major scientist of his time (often referred to as the father of science) and used mathematics to properly describe scientific events. For all of his great efforts, though, as our machines have grown in power, we have had to rethink some of his theories. His improvements on the telescope enabled him to locate and accurately name many planets, stars, and systems. He was unable, however, to correctly ascertain the orbits of planets and the genesis of tides. Sir Isaac Newton expounded upon previous works, including Galileo's, when creating his laws of physics. Thus, tides were finally explained accurately, through an accumulation of knowledge.

Science, mathematics, and technology are intertwined as we can see by observing and understanding the natural world. If we wanted to fully explain an ecosystem, we would need to understand how climate (meteorology) and soil types (geology) influence the plant (botany) and animal (zoology) forms that thrive and how they ultimately return nutrients to the environment (chemistry and math). The description of this ecosystem could become infinitely large if smaller and smaller subsystems within each system is included along with its feedback loops. At the same time, this ecosystem is interacting with other ecosystems.

c. Recognize that when observations do not agree with an accepted scientific theory, either the observations are mistaken or fraudulent, or the accepted theory is erroneous or incorrect

Sir Isaac Newton must have sensed that Galileo's tide theory didn't make sense because it agree with his observations. He had the opportunity, like present day scientists, to review his observations for error, or find a better explanation. One must note, though, that better in this case must be scientifically accurate in order to be impressive to peers specializing in science.

d. Understand that reproducibility of data is critical to the scientific endeavor

In order to have your theory validated and accepted, it must be documented, accurate and clearly derived. This means that another scientist could follow the exact steps you took and recreate your experiment from your notes, find similar data, and draw the same conclusions. In this way the validity of science is substantiated.

e. Recognize that science is a self-correcting process that eventually identifies misconceptions and experimental biases

The scientific process encourages periodic reassessment. The conclusion step allows one to examine the hypothesis as it relates to experimental data. At this point, one can find positive correlations or discord. When results are unexpected, one should revisit all possible sources of error. If an error is not found to explain the results, one can reconsider the hypothesis and also think about other possibilities. This is why experimentation often results in further experimentation.

f. Recognize that an inquiring mind is at the heart of the scientific method and that doing science involves thinking critically about the evidence presented, the usefulness of models, and the limitations of theories

Science is not merely about creating; it is also about assessment and solutions. Science can be thought of as a loop. One questions something, and creates an experiment to study it. One can learn from this evidence, and then ask more questions. In depth learning involves looking at the experimental data from all angles and continuing to seek knowledge. Learning in depth does not occur by looking at something superficially or by taking someone else's data as 'proof.' Go one step further. Analyze the evidence as if you were searching for a problem. Maybe there won't be one, but you will be more likely to find it if there is. Ask questions that start with "How" and "Why" and seek the answers in the data. Question causes and effects to make sure they are correlated.

A model attempts to take the known information and put it together in such a way as to show a "picture" of how those parts work together in nature. It shows the relationship among various parts. Models change when more information becomes available. For example, the model of the atom has gone through several stages: plum pudding, planets and sun, sun with electron clouds. Models that can be shown on the computer have become extremely helpful as they can be manipulated and are very visual representations of real systems.

A theory is a broad generalization that takes the results of several experiments and explains them using a broad, single idea. A hypotheses does not become a theory without many years of testing and trying to disprove it.

g. Recognize that theories are judged by how well they explain observations and predict results and that when they represent new ideas that are counter to mainstream ideas they often encounter vigorous criticism

If a theory explains a phenomenon well, it is worth considering, even if it turns out later to be incorrect. The problem with this is two fold. First, a person can use a theory to push their own beliefs. This is the case with people seeing what they want to see, and then forming theories based on their opinions. An example is ia scientist expecting certain results, and finding ways to skew the results to match his theory. A theory based upon opinions will soon be exposed as transparent and will be dismissed because it has no pertinent data to support it. Even if a theory is developed well, it still may not be readily accepted. A new theory is almost always difficult to introduce to an established community. To have a theory hold up to scrutiny, the author must have accurate data. Second, the author must continue to publicize the information. Just because a theory is not commonplace, does not mean it is incorrect. Novel ideas often become cornerstones of understanding, but it doesn't happen overnight. If the experiment has reproducible results and strong mathematics, it will eventually sway people.

h. Recognize that when observations, data, or experimental results do not agree, the unexpected results are not necessarily mistakes; to discard the unusual in order to reach the expected is to guarantee that nothing but what is expected will ever be seen

Often, results that deviate from the expected are the result of error. However, this is not always the case. Consider a scientist who has double checked his work multiple times and can find no errors. He can not explain what has happened, except to assume that his theory was wrong. Maybe there is a fundamental scientific phenomenon that has yet to be explained and he couldn't possibly have known. Discoveries can occur in this way. If the scientist were to give up, he and society would lose the opportunity to learn something new. If the scientist opens his mind to the discovery, there are limitless possibilities for learning.

i. Know why curiosity, honesty, openness, and skepticism are so highly regarded in science and how they are incorporated into the way science is carried out

Curiosity fuels research. It prompts the questions that turn into scientific inquiry. Honesty is paramount to the scientific method. To put the research out there, and be true in your report of the findings, is to help mankind and cooperate in scientific endeavors. Openness and skepticism are both necessary in the field of research. One should be humble. One should be open to others' ideas, and open to their own unexpected findings, but be critical in evaluation of the work as it was conducted. It is key to incorporate all of these traits and to conduct yourself in a respectable and responsible manner.

Notice: For those of you using the State of California topical guide, please note that they omit letters f and g. XAMonline has taken that fact into account and properly sequenced the letters.

Skill 6.2   Scientific Ethics

To understand scientific ethics, we need to have a clear understanding of general ethics. Ethics is a system of public, general rules for guiding human conduct (Gert, 1988). The rules are general because they apply to all people at all times and they are public because they are not secret codes or practices.

Philosophers have given a number of moral theories to justify moral rules, which range from utilitarianism (a theory of ethics that prescribes the quantitative maximization of good consequences for a population proposed by Mozi, a Chinese philosopher who lived from 471-381 BC,) Kantianism (a theory proposed by Immanuel Kant, a German philosopher who lived from 1724-1804, which ascribes intrinsic value to rational beings and is the philosophical foundation of contemporary human rights) to social contract theory (a view of the ancient Greeks which states that the person's moral and or political obligations are dependent upon a contract or agreement between them to form society).

The following are some of the guiding principles of scientific ethics:

1. Scientific Honesty: refrain from fabricating or misinterpreting data for personal gain
2. Caution: avoid errors and sloppiness in all scientific experimentation
3. Credit: give credit where credit is due and do not copy
4. Responsibility: report reliable information to the public and do not mislead in the name of science
5. Freedom: freedom to criticize old ideas, question new research, and conduct independent research.

a. Understand that honesty is at the core of scientific ethics; first and foremost is the honest and accurate reporting of procedures used and data collected.

Scientists should show good conduct in their scientific pursuits. Conduct here refers to all aspects of scientific activity including experimentation, testing, education, data evaluation, data analysis, data storing, and peer review.

Some scientists feel great pressure to make important discoveries that will garner funding, further their career, or enable them to file a patent, and this clouds their judgment. However, scientists are forced to resign and forfeit their careers if they are found to have published false data. The consequences of fraud are expected to be severe since other scientists worldwide will be utilizing their time and resources to build on the published work.

b. Know that all scientists are obligated to evaluate the safety of an investigation and ensure the safety of those performing the experiment

As a teacher, the safety of your classroom is your responsibility. You should make every effort to ensure students' safety. You will need to be aware of all potential safety concerns. Advance preparation will prepare you to take the necessary precautions related to the specific experiment. You should use the applicable MSDS and check pertinent regulations (at your place of employment as well as on the state/national levels). It will be necessary to take foreseeability and negligence into consideration. It is the responsibility of the scientist to make sure that all organisms associated with the project are kept safe. This refers to both people and animals.

c. Know the procedures for respectful treatment of all living organisms in experimentation and other investigations

No dissections may be performed on living mammalian vertebrates or birds. Lower order life and invertebrates may be used. Biological experiments may be done with all animals except mammalian vertebrates or birds. No physiological harm may result to the animal. All animals housed and cared for in the school must be handled in a safe and humane manner. Animals are not to remain on school premises during extended vacations unless adequate care is provided. Any instructor who intentionally refuses to comply with the laws may be suspended or dismissed.

Pathogenic organisms must never be used for experimentation. Students should adhere to the following rules at all times when working with microorganisms to avoid accidental contamination:

1. Treat all microorganisms as if they were pathogenic.
2. Maintain sterile conditions at all times.

Dissection and alternatives to dissection

Animals which were not obtained from recognized sources should not be used. Decaying animals or those of unknown origin may harbor pathogens and/or parasites. Specimens should be rinsed before handling. Latex gloves are recommended. If not available, students with sores or scratches should be excused from the activity. Formaldehyde is likely carcinogenic and should be avoided or disposed of according to district regulations. Students objecting to dissections for moral reasons should be given an alternative assignment. Interactive dissections are available online or from software companies for those students who object to performing dissections. There should be no penalty for those students who refuse to physically perform a dissection.

Skill 6.3   Historical Perspectives

a. Discuss the cumulative nature of scientific evidence as it relates to the development of models and theories

Science is an ongoing process. There was a time when microscopes, telescopes, calculators, and computers did not exist. Their current availability has led to many discoveries. We have had the opportunity to investigate why people become sick, and the mechanisms responsible for their illnesses. We have also broadened our knowledge of physical science; the laws that govern the universe. With each new breakthrough we either build upon current knowledge, or if the new piece doesn't work with previous thoughts, we reevaluate the validity of all of the information, past and present. For this reason, models and theories are continuously evolving.

The scientific method provides principles and procedures for the systematic pursuit of knowledge involving the recognition and formulation of a problem, the collection of data through observation and experimentation, and the formulation and testing of hypotheses. This process is used to continually test existing theories and revise them over time.

A scientific theory is used to explain an observation or a set of observations. It is generally accepted to be true, though no absolute proof exists. An important feature of a scientific theory is that there are no experimental observations to disprove it, and each piece of evidence that exists supports the theory as written. Theories can be revised over time to include the results of all experimental observations, or even discarded completely if new experimental evidence, accepted by the scientific community, is at odds with the original theory. Theories provide a framework to explain the known information of the time, but are subject to constant evaluation and updating.

Models are created to demonstrate theories in a more concrete way. A good example of theories and models which have changed over the years is the atomic model. Early observations predicted a plum pudding model based on several postulates proposed by Dalton. Thomson refined that model based on his work with electrons. However, the entire model was changed in 1911 when Rutherford discovered that nearly all the mass of an atom is contained in a small, positively charged nucleus. His sun-and-planets theory was further refined by the research of Bohr and DeBroglie. And the idea of precise orbits was replaced by the idea of orbitals with the electrons located within a region. Each theory and model was based on the knowledge that was known at the time. However, as technology progressed and research in other areas provided clues about the atom, the theory and model of the atom was changed to reflect the new knowledge.

b. Recognize that as knowledge in science evolves, when observations do not support an accepted scientific theory, the observations are reconsidered to determine if they are mistaken or fraudulent, or if the accepted theory is erroneous or incomplete (e.g., an erroneous theory is the Piltdown Man fossil; an incomplete theory is Newton's laws of gravity)

When one realizes that their results do not match previously established norms, the new results must be reconsidered. At this point, four possibilities exist to explain the discrepancy. One should look closely at the new results.

The first place for disagreement is the new observations; they may be mistaken. Was there an error in data collection or analysis? Repeating the experiment may yield results that more closely agree with the previous theory. If the results of the follow up experiment are the same, an observer may wonder if the new data is fraudulent (second possibility).

Take for example the scientist who fabricates data, but repeatedly insists on its integrity, even though it contradicts previous studies (remember that having a current study contradict a previous one would be acceptable, providing the results were true and reproducible). Another possibility would be a problem with the previously accepted theory. An erroneous theory is one which was created with misinformation. An example of an erroneous theory would be the Piltdown Man fossil. The Piltdown Man fossil consisted of fragments of a skull and jaw bone collected in the early 1900's from a gravel pit at Piltdown, a village in England. Scientists asserted that this discovery was the fossilized remains of an unknown early form of man. In 1953 it was exposed as a forgery, and properly evaluated as the lower jaw bone of an ape combined with the skull of a fully developed, modern man. There is still some debate as to who created the forgery, but it provided quite a stir in the scientific community.

The problem with an erroneous theory is that it can be believable, and then future assumptions may be based on its inaccuracy. When theories become entrenched this way it is difficult sometimes to go back and locate the error. This can be seen when studying phylogenies. If Piltdown Man was assumed to come from ancestors, and to have generations before him, the accusation of his being fraudulent sheds new light on the phylogenic tree as it was proposed.

A final source for dispute would be that the original theory was incomplete, such as was true with Newton's laws of gravity. Galileo had created an erroneous theory to describe the motion of planets. It was discredited when Sir Isaac Newton established his famous laws of gravity. Newton's concept of gravity held until the beginning of the 20th century, when Einstein proposed his general theory of relativity. The key to Einstein's version is that inertia occurs when objects are in free fall instead of when they are at rest. The theory of general relativity has been well accepted because multiple experiments have repeatedly confirmed its predictions.

c. Recognize and provide specific examples that scientific advances sometimes result in profound paradigm shifts in scientific theories

A paradigm shift is a change in the underlying assumptions that define a particular scientific theory. Scientific advances, such as increased technology allowing different or more reliable data collection, sometimes result in paradigm shifts in scientific theories.

One classic example of a scientific paradigm shift is the transition from a geocentric (Earth-centered) to heliocentric (Sun-centered) model of the universe. Invention and development of the telescope allowed for greater observation of the planets and the Sun. The theory that the Sun is the center of the universe around which the planets, including the Earth, rotate gained acceptance largely because of the advances in observational technology.

Another example of a paradigm shift is the acceptance of plate tectonics as the explanation for large-scale movements in the Earth's crust. Advances in seismic imaging and observation techniques allowed for the collection of sufficient data to establish plate tectonics as a legitimate geological theory.

d. Discuss the need for clear and understandable communication of scientific endeavors so that they may be reproduced and why reproduction of these endeavors is important

Clear and understandable communication is essential for continuity and progress in science. When scientists complete scientific endeavors, such as research experiments, it is important that they carefully record their methods and results. Such precise communication and record keeping allows other scientists to reproduce the experiments in the future.

Reproduction of scientific endeavors is important because it simplifies the verification process. Because scientific experiments are subject to many sources of error, verification of results is essential. Scientists must verify results from scientific endeavors in order to justify the use of the acquired data in developing theories and future experiments.

In addition, clear communication of scientific endeavors allows scientists to learn from the work of others. Such sharing of information speeds the process of scientific research and development.

In earlier times, the lack of communication among scientists often meant that two or more scientists or teams of scientists were working on the exact same problem at the exact same time. With the advent of the printing press and later the telephone and television, it became possible for scientists to have greater connections with each other to understand the work that was already done or in progress on a given problem. As computers and the internet have come into widespread use, scientists from around the world can instantly find others doing the same or similar work and read each others' findings or talk with each other to collaborate instead of working alone and duplicating efforts. However, in the rush to publish, scientists must be very clear in how they present their research and results and must write in such a way as to be understood by others wanting to reproduce and validate the experiment.

Competency 7.0 Science and Society

Skill 7.1   Science Literacy

a. Recognize that science attempts to make sense of how the natural and the designed world function

Human beings reside at the top of the food web for many reasons including physical dexterity and size, but largely because of brain power. We are thinkers, designed to be curious (as are our friends, the primates). Science is our attempt to understand the world around us, and to live within it. Science is not always accurate, and often theories are inadequate, or believed to be true only to be disproven later. Please remember that science is a man-made endeavor, and you and your students should treat it as such.

b. Demonstrate the ability to apply critical and independent thinking to weigh alternative explanations of events

In section 5.3j we demonstrated the importance of assessing the validity of information. One should consider the suggestions given in 5.3j when weighing evidence. Additional information on this subject may be found in Scientific Inquiry, Section 6.1 a-k.

c. Apply evidence, numbers, patterns, and logical arguments to solve problems

Two of the most important aspects of science are data and honesty. In the scientific realm, numbers are stronger than words, so be sure to back up your comments with accurate data and examples. By using the scientific method, you will be more likely to catch mistakes, correct biases, and obtain accurate results. When assessing experimental data utilize the proper tools and mathematical concepts discussed in this guide.

When looking at experimental results, one should always look for patterns. Results should be expressed in numbers whenever possible. The data should be charted and/or graphed in such a way as to show any trends and similarities. All data must be reported in order to see anything that might disprove the idea that the scientist is proposing. Remember that nature, in general, shows great order in its systems, so step back and try to see the "big picture" that the evidence is showing.

d. Understand that, although much has been learned about the objects, events, and phenomena in nature, there are many unanswered questions, i.e., science is a work in progress

The combination of science, mathematics, and technology forms the scientific endeavor and makes science a success. It is impossible to study science on its own without the support of other disciplines like mathematics, technology, geology, physics, and other disciplines. Science is an ongoing process involving multiple fields and individuals. Technology also plays a role in scientific discoveries as we are limited by technology. We are constantly creating new devices for experimentation, and with each one comes new revelations. As such, science is constantly developing. The nature of science consists of three important aspects: the scientific world view, scientific inquiry, and scientific enterprise.

The scientific world view

This includes some very important issues such as the possibility of understanding this highly organized world and its complexities with the help of latest technology. Scientific ideas are subject to change. After repeated experiments, a theory is established, but this theory could be changed in the future. Only laws that occur naturally do not change.

Scientific knowledge is never discarded, but is instead modified – e.g., Albert Einstein didn't discard the Newtonian principles but modified them in his theory of relativity.

In addition, science cannot answer all our questions. We can't find answers to questions related to our beliefs, moral values, and norms.

Scientific inquiry

Scientific inquiry starts with a simple question. This simple question leads to information gathering and an educated guess otherwise known as a hypothesis. To prove the hypothesis, scientists conduct experiments, which yield data and a conclusion. All experiments must be repeated at least twice to get reliable results. Thus, scientific inquiry leads to new knowledge or the verification of established theories.

Science requires proof or evidence. Science depends on accuracy and the absence of bias or prejudice. In science, there is no place for preconceived ideas or premeditated results. By using their senses and modern technology, scientists will be able to gather reliable information.

Science is a combination of logic and imagination. A scientist needs to think, imagine, and be able to reason.

Science explains, reasons, and predicts. These three tasks are interwoven and inseparable. While reasoning is absolutely important for science, there should be no bias or prejudice.

Science is not authoritarian because history has proven that scientific authority is often wrong. Nobody can determine or make decisions for others on any issue.

Scientific enterprise

Science is a complex activity involving various people and places. A scientist may work alone or in a laboratory, classroom, or, for that matter, anywhere. Mostly it is a group activity requiring the social skills of cooperation, communication of results or findings, consultation, and discussion. Science demands a high degree of communication to other scientists, governments, funding authorities, and the public.

e. Know that the ability of science and technology to resolve societal problems depends on the scientific literacy of a society

The most common definitions of science literacy are scientific awareness (Devlin 1998) and scientific ways of knowing (Maienshein 1999). In simple terms, scientific literacy is a combination of concepts, history, and philosophy, which help us to understand the scientific issues of our time. The aim is to have a society that is aware of scientific developments.

Scientific literacy allows members of a society –

1. To understand current terminology and issues
2. To appreciate the role of natural laws in ones life
3. To have an idea of the scientific advances
4. To evaluate scientific information and weigh the risks and benefits of a course of action in the individual's life

We are living in an age of scientific discovery and technology. On TV and in the newspapers, we are constantly fed news related to science and technology. Scientific and technological issues dominate our lives. We need to be scientifically literate to understand these issues. Understanding these debates has become as important as reading and writing. In order to appreciate the world around us and make informed personal decisions, we need to be scientifically literate.

It is the responsibility of the scientific community and educators to help the public cope with the fast-paced changes that are taking place now in the fields of science and technology.

Scientific literacy is based on the understanding of the most general principles and a broad knowledge of science. A society that is scientifically aware possesses facts and vocabulary sufficient to understand the context of the daily news. If one can understand articles about genetic engineering, the ozone hole, and greenhouse effects as well as sports, politics, arts, or the theater, then one is scientifically literate.

As medical care is increasingly in the hands of the person being cared for, the individual must possess a high level of scientific literacy in order to be able to access current information and evaluate various courses of treatment for their risks and benefits in his situation. Ecology and greenhouse effects have come to the forefront of the issues of daily living, so individuals need to avail themselves of the latest information and understand how to act appropriately in light of that information.

Scientific literacy is different from technological literacy. A survey indicated that less than 7% of adults, 22% of college graduates and 26% of those with graduate degrees are scientifically literate. These numbers are not encouraging. In order to rectify this problem, more emphasis has been placed on science education in K-12 and at the college level.

Skill 7.2   Diversity

a. Identify examples of women and men of various social and ethnic backgrounds with diverse interests, talents, qualities, and motivations who are, or who have been, engaged in activities of science and related fields

Curiosity is the heart of science. This is why so many diverse people are drawn to it. In the area of zoology one of the most recognized scientists is Jane Goodall. Goodall is known for her research into social and family interactions of chimpanzees in Africa. Goodall has spent many years abroad conducting long term studies of chimp interactions, and returns from Africa to lecture and provide information about Africa, the chimpanzees, and her institute located in Tanzania. Her work has spawned innovative, community-centered conservation and development programs around the world.

In the area of chemistry we recognize Dorothy Crowfoot Hodgkin. She studied at Oxford and won the Nobel Prize of Chemistry in 1964 for determining the shape of the vitamin B-12. She also determined 3-dimensional structures for cholesterol, penicillin, insulin, tobacco mosaic virus, and several other molecules using X-ray crystallography.

Florence Nightingale was a 19th century nurse who shaped the nursing profession. Nightingale was born into wealth and shocked her family by choosing to study health reforms for the poor in lieu of attending the expected social events. She studied nursing in Paris and became involved in the Crimean War. The British lacked supplies and the secretary of war asked for Nightingale's assistance. She earned her nickname "The Lady with the Lamp" while walking the floors at night checking on patients and writing letters to British officials demanding supplies. Her greatest accomplishment was her reports and statistics that confirmed that unclean living conditions were to blame more often that wounds and disease in the deaths of soldiers during the Crimean War. Along with Elizabeth Blackwell, the first British female physician, she opened the Women's Medical College. By mentoring Linda Richards, "America's first trained nurse," she also established quality nursing schools in the U.S.

George Washington Carver, a black botany researcher and agronomy educator, became known for his work on alternative crops for the South when the soil became depleted from years of growing cotton. His most famous method of promoting peanuts to the farmers involved his creation of over 100 products from peanuts. He continues to serve as a role model of hard work, a positive attitude and a good education.

In 1903, the Nobel Prize in Physics was jointly awarded to three individuals: Marie Curie, Pierre Curie, and Antoine Becquerel for their discovery of radioactivity and some of its uses in medicine. Marie Curie was the first woman ever to receive this prestigious award. In addition, she received the Nobel Prize in chemistry in 1911, making her the only person to receive two Nobel awards in science. Ironically, her cause of death in 1934 was of overexposure to radioactivity, the research for which she was so respected.

Neil Armstrong is an American icon. He will always be symbolically linked to our aeronautics program. An astronaut and naval aviator, he is best known for being the first human to set foot on the Moon. He is well-known for his summation of that accomplishment: "That's one small step for man, one giant leap for mankind."

Sir Alexander Fleming was a pharmacologist from Scotland who isolated the antibiotic penicillin from a mold in 1928. Flemming also noted that bacteria developed resistance whenever too little penicillin was used or when it was used for too short a period, a key problem we still face today.

Skill 7.3 Science, Technology, and Society

a. Identify and evaluate the impact of scientific advances on society

Science and society are interconnected. Important discoveries in science and technology influence society and have the potential to alter society. Society, as a whole, impacts biological research. The pressure from the majority of society has led to bans and restrictions on human cloning research. The United States government and the governments of many other countries have restricted human cloning. The U.S. legislature has banned the use of federal funds for the development of human cloning techniques. Some individual states have banned human cloning regardless of where the funds originate.

The needs of society drive the direction of scientific investigation. The demand for genetically modified crops by society and industry has steadily increased over the years. Genetic engineering in the agricultural field has led to improved crops for human use and consumption. Crops are genetically modified for increased growth and insect resistance because of the demand for larger and greater quantities of produce.

With advances in biotechnology come people in society who oppose it. Ethical questions come into play when discussing animal and human research. Does it need to be done? What are the effects on humans and animals? There are no absolute right or wrong answers to these questions. There are governmental agencies in place to regulate the use of humans and animals for research.

Science and technology are often referred to as a "double-edged sword". Although advances in medicine have greatly improved the quality and length of life, certain moral and ethical controversies have arisen. Unforeseen environmental problems may result from technological advances. Advances in science have led to an improved economy through biotechnology as applied to agriculture, yet it has put our health care system at risk and has caused the cost of medical care to skyrocket. Society depends on science, so it is necessary for the public be scientifically literate and informed in order to allow potentially unethical procedures to occur. Especially vulnerable are the areas of genetic research and fertility. It is important for science teachers to stay abreast of current research and to involve students in critical thinking and ethics whenever possible.

c. Recognize that scientific advances may challenge individuals to reevaluate their personal beliefs

It is easy to say one is for or against something. Biotechnological advances are reaching new heights. This is both exciting and, to some, it is frightening. We are stretching our boundaries and rethinking old standards. Things we never thought possible, such as the human genome project, now seem ordinary, and cloning, once in the realm of science fiction, is now available. These revelations force us to rethink our stance on issues.

Before taking a stand on a scientific issue, one should do as much reading and research on the subject as possible to understand all the angles and implications as well as the motives for the scientific issue. That requires research skills, critical thinking skills, scientific literacy, and often interaction with others. It also means the person must know his own belief system and morals so that he has something to judge the scientific advance against.

Risks and benefits also become important issues when evaluating the usefulness of a scientific advancement. In the case of risks and benefits, the risks for one person may outweigh the benefits but for another person the benefits may far outweigh the risks. Therefore, a risk-benefit analysis is both individual and societal.

It is normal to reevaluate one's beliefs. Reevaluation requires truly thinking about a topic, which in turn allows for recommitment to a topic or, possibly, a new, well thought out position.

Skill 7.4   Safety

a. Choose appropriate safety equipment for a given activity (e.g., goggles, apron, vented hood)

It is the responsibility of the teacher to provide a safe environment for his or her students. Proper supervision greatly reduces the risk of injury and a teacher should never leave a class for any reason without providing alternate supervision. After an accident, two factors are considered, **foreseeability** and **negligence**. Foreseeability is the anticipation that an event could occur under certain circumstances. Negligence is the failure to exercise ordinary or reasonable care. Safety procedures should be a part of the science curriculum and a well managed classroom is important to avoid potential lawsuits.

Students should wear safety goggles when performing dissections, heating, or while using acids and bases. Hair should always be tied back and objects should never be placed in the mouth. Food should not be consumed while in the laboratory. Hands should always be washed before and after laboratory experiments. In case of an accident, eye washes and showers should be used for eye contamination or a chemical spill that covers the student's body. Small chemical spills should only be contained and cleaned by the teacher. Kitty litter or a chemical spill kit should be used to clean a spill. For large spills, the school administration and the local fire department should be notified. Biological spills should only be handled by the teacher. Contamination with biological waste can be cleaned by using bleach when appropriate. Accidents and injuries should always be reported to the school administration and local health facilities. The severity of the accident or injury will determine the course of action.

b. Discuss the safe use, storage, and disposal of commonly used chemicals and biological specimens

All laboratory solutions should be prepared as directed in the lab manual. Care should be taken to avoid contamination. All glassware should be rinsed thoroughly with distilled water before using and cleaned well after use. All solutions should be made with distilled water as tap water contains dissolved particles that may affect the results of an experiment. Unused solutions should be disposed of according to local disposal procedures.

The "Right to Know Law" covers science teachers who work with potentially hazardous chemicals. Briefly, the law states that employees must be informed of potentially toxic chemicals. An inventory must be made available if requested. The inventory must contain information about the hazards and properties of the chemicals. This inventory is to be checked against the "Substance List". Training must be provided on safe handling and interpretation of the Material Safety Data Sheet.

The following chemicals are potential carcinogens and not allowed in school facilities: Acrylonitriel, Arsenic compounds, Asbestos, Bensidine, Benzene, Cadmium compounds, Chloroform, Chromium compounds, Ethylene oxide, Ortho-toluidine, Nickle powder, and Mercury.

Chemicals should not be stored on bench tops or near heat sources. They should be stored in groups based on their reactivity with one another (such as Acids, Bases, Flammables, Peroxide-forming, Water-reactive, Oxidizers, and Toxins) and in protective storage cabinets with appropriate labeling. All containers within the lab must be labeled. Suspected and known carcinogens must be labeled as such and stored in trays to contain leaks and spills.

Chemical waste should be disposed of in properly labeled containers. Waste should be separated based on its reactivity with other chemicals.

Biological material should never be stored near food or water used for human consumption. All biological material should be appropriately labeled. All blood and body fluids should be put in a well-contained container with a secure lid to prevent leaking. All biological waste should be disposed of in biological hazardous waste bags.

Material safety data sheets are available for every chemical and biological substance. These are available directly from the distribution company and the internet. Before using lab equipment, all lab workers should read and understand the equipment manuals.

c. Assess the safety conditions needed to maintain a science laboratory (e.g., eye wash, shower, fire extinguisher)

All science labs should contain the following **safety equipment**.

-Fire blanket that is visible and accessible.
-Ground Fault Circuit Interrupters (GFCI) within two feet of water supplies
-Signs designating room exits.
-Emergency shower providing a continuous flow of water.
-Emergency eye wash station that can be activated by the foot or forearm.
-Eye protection for every student.
-A means of sanitizing equipment.
-Emergency exhaust fans providing ventilation to the outside of the building.
-Master cut-off switches for gas, electric, and compressed air. Switches must have permanently attached handles. Cut-off switches must be clearly labeled.
-An ABC fire extinguisher.
-Storage cabinets for flammable materials.
-Chemical spill control kit.
-Fume hood with a motor that is spark proof.
-Protective laboratory aprons made of flame retardant material.
-Signs that will alert of potential hazardous conditions.
-Labeled containers for broken glassware, flammables, corrosives, and waste.

d. Read and decode MSDS/OSHA (Material Safety Data Sheet/Occupational Safety and Health Administration) labels on laboratory supplies and equipment

In addition to the safety laws set forth by the government regarding equipment necessary in the lab, OSHA (Occupational Safety and Health Administration) has helped to make environments safer by instituting signs that are bilingual. These signs use pictures rather than or in addition to words and feature eye-catching colors. Some of the best known examples are exit, restrooms, and handicap accessible signs.

Of particular importance to laboratories are diamond safety signs, prohibitive signs, and triangle danger signs. Each sign includes a descriptive picture.

As a teacher, you should utilize a MSDS (Material Safety Data Sheet) whenever you are preparing an experiment. It is designed to provide people with the proper procedures for handling or working with a particular substance. MSDS's include information such as physical data (melting point, boiling point, etc.), toxicity, health effects, first aid, reactivity, storage, disposal, protective gear, and spill/leak procedures. These are particularly important if a spill or other accident occurs. You should review a few, commonly available online, and understand the listing procedures.

e. Discuss key issues in the disposal of hazardous materials in either the laboratory or the local community

Hazardous materials should never be disposed of with regular trash. Hazardous materials include many cleansers, paints, batteries, oil, and biohazardous products. Labels which caution one to wear gloves, never place item near…, or use in a well ventilated area…, should be taken as signals that the item is hazardous. Often the label will contain a signal word such as "Danger!" or "Caution." It may also contain precautionary measures and first aid information. Disposal of waste down the sink or in regular trash receptacles means that it will eventually enter the water/sewer system or ground, where it could cause contamination. Liquid remains/spills should be solidified using cat litter and then disposed of carefully. Sharps bins are used for the disposal of sharp objects and glass. Red biohazard bags/containers are used for the disposal of biohazard refuse. Your school system and/or local fire department can advise you on their disposal policies and procedures as this may vary from place to place.

f. Be familiar with standard safety procedures such as those outlined in the Science Safety Handbook for California Schools (1999)

Standard safety precautions include wearing gloves, using protective eye wear, and conducting experiments in appropriate areas (ventilated hoods when necessary) with appropriate equipment. The state of California has published a document entitled *Science Safety Handbook for California Schools.* This handbook can be purchased or printed at
http://www.cde.ca.gov/pd/ca/sc/documents/scisafebk.pdf#search=%22CA%20science%20safety%20book%20for%20CA%20schools%22.

Sample Essays

1. Using your accumulated knowledge, discuss the components of biogeochemical cycles.

Best:

Essential elements are recycled through an ecosystem. At times, the element needs to be made available in a useable form. Cycles are dependent on plants, algae, and bacteria to fix nutrients for use by animals. The four main cycles are: water, carbon, nitrogen, and phosphorous.

Two percent of all the water is fixed in ice or the bodies of organisms, rendering it unavailable. Available water includes surface water (lakes, ocean, and rivers) and ground water (aquifers, wells). The majority (96%) of all available water is from ground water. Water is recycled through the processes of evaporation and precipitation. The water present now is the water that has been here since our atmosphere was formed.

Ten percent of all available carbon in the air (in the form of carbon dioxide gas) is fixed by photosynthesis. Plants fix carbon in the form of glucose. Animals eat the plants and are able to obtain the carbon necessary to sustain themselves. When animals release carbon dioxide through respiration, the cycle begins again as plants recycle the carbon through photosynthesis.

Eighty percent of the atmosphere is in the form of nitrogen gas. Nitrogen must be fixed and taken out of the gaseous form to be incorporated into an organism. Only a few genera of bacteria have the correct enzymes to break the strong triple bond between nitrogen atoms. These special bacteria live within the roots of legumes (e.g., peas, beans, alfalfa) and add bacteria to the soil so it may be taken-up by the plant. Nitrogen is necessary in the building of amino acids and the nitrogenous bases of DNA.

Phosphorus exists as a mineral and is not found in the atmosphere. Fungi and plant roots have structures called mycorrhizae that are able to fix insoluble phosphates into useable phosphorus. Urine and decayed matter returns phosphorus to the earth where it can be fixed in the plant. Phosphorus is needed for the backbone of DNA and for the manufacture of ATP.

The four biogeochemical cycles are present concurrently. Water is continually recycled, and is utilized by organisms to sustain life. Carbon is also a necessary component for life. Both water and carbon can be found in the air and on the ground. Nitrogen and phosphorous are commonly found in the ground. Special organisms, called decomposers, help to make these elements available in the environment. Plants use the recycled materials for energy and, when they are consumed, the cycle begins again.

Better:

Essential elements are recycled through an ecosystem. Cycles are dependent on plants, algae, and bacteria to make nutrients available for use by animals. The four main cycles are: water, carbon, nitrogen, and phosphorous. Water is typically available as surface water (large bodies of water) or ground water. Water is recycled through the states of gas, liquid (rain), and solid (ice or snow). Carbon is necessary for life as it is the basis for organic matter. It is a byproduct of photosynthesis and is found in the air as carbon dioxide gas. Nitrogen is the largest component of the atmosphere. It is also necessary for the creation of amino acids and the nitrogenous bases of DNA. Phosphorous is another elemental cycle. Phosphorous is found in the soil and is made available by decomposition. It is then converted for use in the manufacture of DNA and ATP.

Basic:

Elements are recycled through an ecosystem. This occurs through cycles. These important cycles are called biogeochemical cycles. The water cycle consists of water moving from bodies of water into the air and back again as precipitation. The carbon cycle includes all organisms, as mammals breathe out carbon dioxide and are made of carbon molecules. Nitrogen is an amino acid building block and is found in soil. As things are broken down, phosphorous is added to the earth, enriching the soil.

2. Examine the components of a eukaryotic cell.

Best:

The cell is the basic unit of all living things. Eukaryotic cells are found in protists, fungi, plants, and animals. Eukaryotic cells are organized. They contain many organelles, which are membrane bound areas for specific functions. Their cytoplasm contains a cytoskeleton that provides a protein framework for the cell. The cytoplasm also supports the organelles and contains the ions and molecules necessary for cell function. The cytoplasm is contained by the plasma membrane. The plasma membrane allows molecules to pass in and out of the cell. The membrane can bud inward to engulf outside material in a process called endocytosis. Exocytosis is a secretory mechanism, the reverse of endocytosis.

Eukaryotes have a nucleus. The nucleus is the brain of the cell that contains all of the cell's genetic information. The genetic information is contained on chromosomes that consist of chromatin, which are complexes of DNA and proteins. The chromosomes are tightly coiled to conserve space while providing a large surface area. The nucleus is the site of transcription of the DNA into RNA. The nucleolus is where ribosomes are made. There is at least one of these dark-staining bodies inside the nucleus of most eukaryotes.

The nuclear envelope is two membranes separated by a narrow space. The envelope contains many pores that let RNA out of the nucleus.

Ribosomes are the site for protein synthesis. They may be free floating in the cytoplasm or attached to the endoplasmic reticulum. There may be up to a half a million ribosomes in a cell, depending on how much protein the cell makes.

The endoplasmic reticulum (ER) is folded and provides a large surface area. It is the "roadway" of the cell and allows for transport of materials through and out of the cell. There are two types of ER: smooth and rough. Smooth endoplasmic reticulum contains no ribosomes on their surface. This is the site of lipid synthesis. Rough endoplasmic reticulum has ribosomes on its surfaces. They aid in the synthesis of proteins that are membrane bound or destined for secretion.

Many of the products made in the ER proceed to the Golgi apparatus. The Golgi apparatus functions to sort, modify, and package molecules that are made in the other parts of the cell. These molecules are either sent out of the cell or to other organelles within the cell. The Golgi apparatus is a stacked structure to increase the surface area.

Lysosomes are found mainly in animal cells. These contain digestive enzymes that break down food, unnecessary substances, viruses, damaged cell components, and eventually the cell itself. It is believed that lysosomes play a role in the aging process.

Mitochondria are large organelles that are the site of cellular respiration, where ATP is made to supply energy to the cell. Muscle cells have many mitochondria because they use a great deal of energy. Mitochondria have their own DNA, RNA, and ribosomes and are capable of reproducing by binary fission if there is a great demand for additional energy. Mitochondria have two membranes: a smooth outer membrane and a folded inner membrane. The folds inside the mitochondria are called cristae. They provide a large surface area for cellular respiration to occur.

Plastids are found only in photosynthetic organisms. They are similar to the mitochondira due to the double membrane structure. They also have their own DNA, RNA, and ribosomes and can reproduce if the need for the increased capture of sunlight becomes necessary. There are several types of plastids. Chloroplasts are the sight of photosynthesis. The stroma is the chloroplast's inner membrane space. The stoma encloses sacs called thylakoids that contain the photosynthetic pigment chlorophyll. The chlorophyll traps sunlight inside the thylakoid to generate ATP which is used in the stroma to produce carbohydrates and other products. The chromoplasts make and store yellow and orange pigments. They provide color to leaves, flowers, and fruits. The amyloplasts store starch and are used as a food reserve. They are abundant in roots like potatoes.

The Endosymbiotic Theory states that mitochondria and chloroplasts were once free living and possibly evolved from prokaryotic cells. At some point in our evolutionary history, they entered the eukaryotic cell and maintained a symbiotic relationship with the cell, with both the cell and organelle benefiting from the relationship. The fact that they both have their own DNA, RNA, ribosomes, and are capable of reproduction helps to confirm this theory.

Found in plant cells only, the cell wall is composed of cellulose and fibers. It is thick enough for support and protection, yet porous enough to allow water and dissolved substances to enter. Vacuoles are found mostly in plant cells. They hold stored food and pigments. Their large size allows them to fill with water in order to provide turgor pressure. Lack of turgor pressure causes a plant to wilt.

The cytoskeleton, found in both animal and plant cells, is composed of protein filaments attached to the plasma membrane and organelles. They provide a framework for the cell and aid in cell movement. They constantly change shape and move about. Three types of fibers make up the cytoskeleton:

1. Microtubules – the largest of the three, they make up cilia and flagella for locomotion. Some examples are sperm cells, cilia that line the fallopian tubes, and tracheal cilia. Centrioles are also composed of microtubules. They aid in cell division to form the spindle fibers that pull the cell apart into two new cells. Centrioles are not found in the cells of higher plants.

2. Intermediate filaments – intermediate in size, they are smaller than microtubules but larger than microfilaments. They help the cell to keep its shape.

3. Microfilaments – smallest of the three, they are made of actin and small amounts of myosin (like in muscle tissue). They function in cell movement like cytoplasmic streaming, endocytosis, and ameboid movement. This structure pinches the two cells apart after cell division, forming two new cells.

Better:

The cell is the basic unit of all living things. Eukaryotic cells are found in protists, fungi, plants, and animals. Eukaryotic cells are organized. Their cytoplasm contains a cytoskeleton that provides a protein framework for the cell. The cytoplasm is contained by the plasma membrane. The plasma membrane allows molecules to pass in and out of the cell.

Eukaryotes have a nucleus. The nucleus is the brain of the cell that contains all of the cell's genetic information. The chromosomes house genetic information and are tightly coiled to conserve space while providing a large surface area.

The nucleus is the site of transcription of the DNA into RNA. The nucleolus is where ribosomes are made.

Ribosomes are the site for protein synthesis. There may be up to a half a million ribosomes in a cell, depending on how much protein is made by the cell.

The endoplasmic reticulum (ER) is folded and provides a large surface area. It is the "roadway" of the cell and allows for transport of materials through and out of the cell. It may be smooth or rough.

Many of the products made in the ER proceed to the Golgi apparatus. The Golgi apparatus functions to sort, modify, and package molecules that are made in the other parts of the cell.

Mitochondria are large organelles that are the site of cellular respiration, where ATP is made to supply energy to the cell. Mitochondria have their own DNA, RNA, and ribosomes and are capable of reproducing by binary fission if there is a greater demand for additional energy.

Plastids are found only in photosynthetic organisms. They are similar to the mitochondria. They also have their own DNA, RNA, and ribosomes and can reproduce if the need for an increased capture of sunlight becomes necessary.

Found in plant cells only, the cell wall is composed of cellulose and fibers. It is thick enough for support and protection, yet porous enough to allow water and dissolved substances to enter.

The cytoskeleton, found in both animal and plant cells, is composed of protein filaments attached to the plasma membrane and organelles. They provide a framework for the cell and aid in cell movement. They constantly change shape and move about. Three types of fibers make up the cytoskeleton (in order of size, largest to smallest): microtubules, intermediate filaments, and microfilaments.

Basic:

The cell is the basic unit of all living things. Eukaryotic cells contain many organelles. Eukaryotes have a nucleus. The nucleus is the brain of the cell that contains all of the cell's genetic information. The nucleus is the site of DNA transcription. There is at least one nucleolus inside the nucleus of most eukaryotes. Ribosomes are the site for protein synthesis and can be found on the endoplasmic reticulum (ER). The Golgi apparatus functions to sort, modify, and package molecules that are made in the other parts of the cell. Mitochondria are large organelles that are the site of cellular respiration, where ATP is made to supply energy to the cell.

In plant cells, the cell wall is composed of cellulose and fibers. The cytoskeleton, found in both animal and plant cells, is composed of protein filaments. The three types of fibers differ in size and help the cell to keep its shape and aid in movement.

3. Discuss the scientific process.

Best:

Science is a body of knowledge that is systematically derived from study, observations, and experimentation. Its goal is to identify and establish principles and theories that may be applied to solve problems.

Scientific experimentation must be repeatable. Experimentation leads to theories that can be disproved and are changeable. Science depends on communication, agreement, and disagreement among scientists. It is composed of theories, laws, and hypotheses.

A theory is the formation of principles or relationships that have been verified and accepted.

A law is an explanation of events that occur with uniformity under the same conditions (e.g., laws of nature, law of gravitation).

A hypothesis is an unproved theory or educated guess followed by research to best explain a phenomenon. A theory is a hypothesis that ,after many experiments to attempt to disprove it, has not been disproven.

Science is limited by the available technology. Science is also limited by the data that we can collect. Data may be interpreted differently on different occasions. Science limitations cause explanations to be changeable as new technologies emerge.

The first step in scientific inquiry is posing a question. Next, a hypothesis is formed to provide a plausible explanation. An experiment is then proposed, designed and performed to test this hypothesis. A comparison between the predicted and observed results is the next step. Conclusions are then formed and it is determined whether the hypothesis is correct or incorrect. If incorrect, the next step is to form a new hypothesis and repeat the process.

Better:

Science is derived from study, observations, and experimentation. The goal of science is to identify and establish principles and theories that may be applied to solve problems. Scientific theory and experimentation must be repeatable. It is also possible to disprove or change a theory. Science depends on communication, agreement, and disagreement among scientists. It is composed of theories, laws, and hypotheses.

A theory is a principle or relationship that has been verified and accepted through experiments. A law is an explanation of events that occur with uniformity under the same conditions. A hypothesis is an educated guess followed by research. A theory is a proven hypothesis.

Science is limited by the available technology. The first step in scientific inquiry is posing a question. Next, a hypothesis is formed to provide a plausible explanation. An experiment is then proposed and performed to test this hypothesis. A comparison between the predicted and observed results is the next step. Conclusions are then formed and it is determined whether the hypothesis is correct or incorrect. If incorrect, the next step is to form a new hypothesis and repeat the process.

Basic:

Science is composed of theories, laws, and hypotheses. The first step in scientific inquiry is posing a question. Next, a hypothesis is formed to provide a plausible explanation. An experiment is then proposed and performed to test this hypothesis. A comparison between the predicted and observed results is the next step. Conclusions are then formed and it is determined whether the hypothesis is correct or incorrect. If incorrect, the next step is to form a new hypothesis and repeat the process. Science is always limited by the available technology.

Sample Test

Directions: Read each item and select the best response.

1. **Which is not true about a cell membrane? (Skill 1.1)(Moderate Rigor)**

   A. It is made from phospholipids
   B. Both plant and animal cells have a cell membrane.
   C. The cell wall is the same as the cell membrane in plants.
   D. It controls the passage of nutrients within a cell.

2. **Microorganisms use all but the following to move: (Skill 1.1) (Moderate Rigor)**

   A. Pseudopods
   B. Flagella
   C. Cilia
   D. Pili

3. **Eukaryotic cells are found in all but the following :(Skill 1.1)(Moderate Rigor)**

   A. Bacteria
   B. Protists
   C. Fungi
   D. Animals

4. **Which kingdom is comprised of organisms made of one cell with no nuclear membrane? (Skill 1.1)(Easy Rigor)**

   A. Monera
   B. Protista
   C. Fungi
   D. Algae

5. **Rough endoplasmic reticulum contains: (Skill 1.1)(Moderate Rigor)**

   A. Vacuoles
   B. Mitochondria
   C. Microfilaments
   D. Ribosomes

6. **Identify the correct sequence of organization of living things. (Skill 1.1)(Moderate Rigor)**

   A. cell – organelle – organ – tissue – organ system – organism
   B. cell – tissue – organ – organelle – organ system – organism
   C. organelle – cell – tissue – organ – organ system – organism
   D. organ system – tissue – organelle – cell – organism – organ

7. **Which is not a characteristic of living things?(Skill 1.1)(Easy Rigor)**

   A. movement
   B. cellular structure
   C. metabolism
   D. reproduction

8. **The purpose of the Golgi Apparatus is: (Skill 1.1)(Moderate Rigor)**

   A. To break down proteins
   B. To sort, modify and package molecules
   C. To break down fats
   D. To make carbohydrates.

9. The amyloplasts: (Skill 1.1)(Moderate Rigor)

   A. Store starch in a plant cell
   B. Store waste in animal cells
   C. Store green and yellow pigment
   D. Aid in photosynthesis.

10. The largest of the three fibers found in cells are called: (Skill 1.1)(Moderate Rigor)

   A. Intermediate filaments
   B. Microtubules
   C. Microfilaments
   D. Filaments

11. The Archaea organisms are all but the following: (Skill 1.1)(Rigorous)

   A. Methanogens
   B. Halobacteria
   C. Thermoacidophiles
   D. Bacteriophiles

12. The first cells that evolved on earth were probably of which type?(Skill 1.1)(Moderate Rigor)

   A. autotrophs
   B. eukaryotes
   C. heterotrophs
   D. prokaryotes

13. Oxygen is given off in the... (Skill 1.1)(Moderate Rigor)
   A. light reactions of photosynthesis.
   B. dark reactions of photosynthesis.
   C. Krebs cycle.
   D. reduction of NAD+ to NADH.

14. Bacteria commonly reproduce by a process called binary fission. Which of the following best defines this process? (Skill 1.1)(Rigorous)

   A. viral vectors carry DNA to new bacteria
   B. DNA from one bacterium enters another
   C. DNA doubles and the bacterial cell divides
   D. DNA from dead cells is absorbed into bacteria

15. The shape of a cell depends on its... (Skill 1.1)(Easy Rigor)

   A. function.
   B. structure.
   C. age.
   D. size.

16. The individual parts of cells are best studied using a(n)... (Skill 1.1)(Moderate Rigor)

   A. ultracentrifuge.
   B. phase-contrast microscope.
   C. CAT scan.
   D. electron microscope.

17. Thermoacidophiles are... (Skill 1.1)(Moderate Rigor)

   A. prokaryotes.
   B. eukaryotes.
   C. bacteria.
   D. archaea.

18. Which of the following is not a type of fiber that makes up the cytoskeleton? (Skill 1.1)(Moderate Rigor)

A. vacuoles
B. microfilaments
C. microtubules
D. intermediate filaments

19. Viruses are made of... (Skill 1.1)(Moderate Rigor)

A. a protein coat surrounding a nucleic acid.
B. DNA, RNA, and a cell wall.
C. a nucleic acid surrounding a protein coat.
D. protein surrounded by DNA.

20. Protists are classified into major groups according to... (Skill 1.1)(Moderate Rigor)

A. their method of obtaining nutrition.
B. reproduction.
C. metabolism.
D. their form and function.

21. This stage of mitosis includes cytokinesis or division of the cytoplasm and its organelles.(Skill 1.2)(Rigorous)

A. anaphase
B. interphase
C. prophase
D. telophase

22. Replication of chromosomes occurs during which phase of the cell cycle?(Skill 1.2)(Moderate Rigor)

A. prophase
B. interphase
C. metaphase
D. anaphase

23. Which statement regarding mitosis is correct?(Skill 1.2)(Moderate Rigor)

A. diploid cells produce haploid cells for sexual reproduction
B. sperm and egg cells are produced
C. diploid cells produce diploid cells for growth and repair
D. it allows for greater genetic diversity

24. In a plant cell, telophase is described as...(Skill 1.2)(Moderate Rigor)

A. the time of chromosome doubling.
B. cell plate formation.
C. the time when crossing over occurs.
D. cleavage furrow formation.

25. **Identify this stage of mitosis. (Skill 1.2)(Moderate Rigor)**

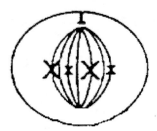

A. anaphase
B. metaphase
C. telophase
D. prophase

26. **Identify this stage of mitosis. (Skill 1.2)(Moderate Rigor)**

A. prophase
B. telophase
C. anaphase
D. metaphase

27. **Which process(es) result(s) in a haploid chromosome number? (Skill 1.2)(Moderate Rigor)**

A. both meiosis and mitosis
B. mitosis
C. meiosis
D. replication and division

28. **Identify this stage of mitosis. (Skill 1.2)(Moderate Rigor)**

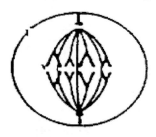

A. anaphase
B. metaphase
C. prophase
D. telophase

29. **Which of the following is a monomer?(Skill 1.3)(Moderate Rigor)**

A. RNA
B. glycogen
C. DNA
D. amino acid

30. **Which does not affect enzyme rate?(Skill 1.3)(Moderate Rigor)**

A. increase of temperature
B. amount of substrate
C. pH
D. size of the cell

31. **All but which one of the following are true of a cell membrane: (Skill 1.3)(Moderate Rigor)**

A. It contains polar and nonpolar phospholipids
B. It only uses active transport to transport molecules across the membrane.
C. It contains cholesterol
D. It has proteins imbedded in it.

32. **Facilitated diffusion: (Skill 1.3)
(Moderate Rigor)**

    A. Requires energy
    B. Only happens in plant cells
    C. Requires a transport molecule to pass through the membrane.
    D. Only allows molecules to leave a cell but not to enter it.

33. **The fluidity of the cell membrane is determined by: (Skill 1.3)(Rigorous)**

    A. Cholesterol
    B. Phospholipids
    C. Imbedded Proteins
    D. DNA

34. **What is not true of enzymes? (Skill 1.3)(Moderate Rigor)**

    A. They are the most diverse of all proteins.
    B. They act on a substrate.
    C. They work at a wide range of pH.
    D. They are temperature-dependent.

35. **What is necessary for diffusion to occur?(Skill 1.3)(Moderate Rigor)**

    A. carrier proteins
    B. energy
    C. a concentration gradient
    D. a membrane

36. **Which is an example of the use of energy to move a substance through a membrane from areas of low concentration to areas of high concentration?(Skill 1.3)(Easy Rigor)**

    A. osmosis
    B. active transport
    C. exocytosis
    D. phagocytosis

37. **A plant cell is placed in salt water. The resulting movement of water out of the cell is called...(Skill 1.3)(Easy Rigor)**

    A. facilitated diffusion.
    B. diffusion.
    C. transpiration.
    D. osmosis.

38. **What are the monomers in polysaccharides? (Skill 1.3)(Moderate rigor)**

    A. Nucleotides
    B. Amino acids
    C. Polypeptides
    D. Simple sugars

39. **A type of molecule not found in the membrane of an animal cell is...(Skill 1.3)(Moderate Rigor)**

    A. phospholipid.
    B. protein.
    C. cellulose.
    D. cholesterol.

40. **Which type of cell would contain the most mitochondria?(Skill 1.3)(Easy Rigor)**

    A. muscle cell
    B. nerve cell
    C. epithelium
    D. blood cell

41. **According to the fluid-mosaic model of the cell membrane, membranes are composed of...(Skill 1.3)(Rigorous)**

    A. phospholipid bilayers with proteins embedded in the layers.
    B. one layer of phospholipids with cholesterol embedded in the layer.
    C. two layers of protein with lipids embedded in the layers.
    D. DNA and fluid proteins.

42. **All the following statements regarding both a mitochondria and a chloroplast are correct except...(Skill 1.3)(Moderate Rigor)**

    A. they both produce energy over a gradient.
    B. they both have DNA and are capable of reproduction.
    C. they both transform light energy to chemical energy.
    D. they both make ATP.

43. **Which is the correct statement regarding the human nervous system and the human endocrine system?(Skill 1.3)(Moderate Rigor)**

    A. the nervous system maintains homeostasis whereas the endocrine system does not
    B. endocrine glands produce neurotransmitters whereas nerves produce hormones
    C. nerve signals travel on neurons whereas hormones travel through the blood
    D. the nervous system involves chemical transmission whereas the endocrine system does not

44. **The most ATP is generated through...(Skill 1.3)(Moderate Rigor)**

    A. fermentation.
    B. glycolysis.
    C. chemiosmosis.
    D. the Krebs cycle.

45. **The function of the cardiovascular system is to: (Skill 1.4)(Moderate Rigor)**

    A. Move oxygenated blood around the body via a pump and tubes

    B. To oxygenate the blood through gas exchange.

    C. To act as an exocrine system

    D. To flush toxins out of the body

46. **Parts of the nervous system include all but the following: (Skill 1.4)(Easy Rigor)**

    A. brain

    B. spinal cord

    C. axons

    D. venules

47. **Homeostatic mechanisms in the body include all but the following: (Skill 1.4)(Moderate Rigor)**

    A. Thermoregulation

    B. Excretion

    C. Respiration

    D. Osmoregulation

48. **The body's endocrine mechanisms are controlled by: (Skill 1.4) (Moderate Rigor)**

    A. Feedback loops

    B. Control molecules

    C. Neurochemicals

    D. Neurotransmitters

49. **The gland that regulated the calcium in the body is the: (Skill 1.4)(Moderate Rigor)**

    A. Thyroid gland

    B. Parathyroid gland

    C. Hypothalamus

    D. Pituitary gland

50. **What is not one of the three gonadal steroids? (Skill 1.4)(Rigorous)**

    A. Testosterone

    B. Estrogen

    C. Progesterone

    D. ACTH

51. **The most common neurotransmitter is: (Skill 1.4)(Moderate Rigor)**

    A. epinephrine

    B. serotonin

    C. Acetyl choline

    D. norepinephrine

52. **Food is carried through the digestive tract by a series of wave-like contractions. This process is called... (Skill 1.4)(Easy Rigor)**

    A. peristalsis.
    B. chyme.
    C. digestion.
    D. absorption.

53. **Movement is possible by the action of muscles pulling on... (Skill 1.4)(Moderate Rigor)**

    A. skin.
    B. bones.
    C. joints.
    D. ligaments.

54. All of the following are functions of the skin except... (Skill 1.4)(Easy Rigor)

    A. storage.
    B. protection.
    C. sensation.
    D. regulation of temperature.

55. Hormones are essential to the regulation of reproduction. What organ is responsible for the release of hormones for sexual maturity? (Skill 1.4)(Moderate Rigor)

    A. pituitary gland
    B. hypothalamus
    C. pancreas
    D. thyroid gland

56. A bicyclist has a heart rate of 110 beats per minute and a stroke volume of 85 mL per beat. What is the cardiac output?(Skill 1.4)(Rigorous)

    A. 9.35 L/min
    B. 1.29 L/min
    C. 0.772 L/min
    D. 129 L/min

57. The type of muscle in the human body that is voluntary is called: (Skill 1.4)(Easy Rigor)

    A. Cardiac

    B. Sarcomere

    C. Smooth

    D. Skeletal

58. The wrist is an example of what kind of joint. (Skill 1.4)(Moderate Rigor)

    A. Ball and socket

    B. Pivot

    C. Stationary

    D. Hinge

59. The waterproofing protein in the skin is called: (Skill 1.4) (Rigorous)

    A. keratin

    B. epidermis

    C. collagen

    D. Sebum

60. A muscular adaptation to move food through the digestive system is called... (Skill 1.4)(Easy Rigor)

    A. peristalsis.
    B. passive transport.
    C. voluntary action.
    D. bulk transport.

61. The role of neurotransmitters in nerve action is...(Skill 1.4) (Easy Rigor)

    A. to turn off the sodium pump.
    B. to turn off the calcium pump.
    C. to send impulses to neurons.
    D. to send impulses to the body.

62. Fats are broken down by which substance?(Skill 1.4)(Moderate Rigor)

    A. bile produced in the gall bladder
    B. lipase produced in the gall bladder
    C. glucagons produced in the liver
    D. bile produced in the liver

63. Fertilization in humans usually occurs in the... (Skill 1.4)(Easy Rigor)

    A. uterus.
    B. ovary.
    C. fallopian tubes.
    D. vagina.

64. All of the following are found in the dermis layer of skin except... (Skill 1.4)(Moderate Rigor)

    A. sweat glands.
    B. keratin.
    C. hair follicles.
    D. blood vessels.

65. A school age boy had the chicken pox as a baby. He will most likely not get this disease again because of... (Skill 1.5)(Moderate Rigor)

    A. passive immunity.
    B. vaccination.
    C. antibiotics.
    D. active immunity.

66. Vaccines are available for all but the following: (Skill 1.5)(Easy Rigor)

    A. Mumps

    B. Tetanus

    C. Staphylococcus

    D. Measles

67. Immune defensive components in the body include all but: (Skill 1.5)(Rigorous)

    A. humoral immunity

    B. skin barrier

    C. Blood brain barrier

    D. cell mediated immunity

68. Any foreign particle that causes an immune reaction is: (Skill 1.5)(Moderate Rigor)

    A. an antigen

    B. a histocompatibity complex

    C. as ntibody

    D. a vaccine

69. What is responsible for organ transplantation rejection? (Skill 1.5)(Moderate Rigor)

    A. Antibodies

    B. Major Histocompatibility Complex

    C. Cytotoxic T Cells

    D. Autoimmune factor

70. **Which of the following is not posttranscriptional processing?(Skill 2.1)(Rigorous)**

    A. 5' capping
    B. intron splicing
    C. polypeptide splicing
    D. 3' polyadenylation

71. **The polymerase chain reaction...(Skill 2.1)(Moderate Rigor)**

    A. is a group of polymerases.
    B. is a technique for amplifying DNA.
    C. is a primer for DNA synthesis.
    D. is synthesis of polymerase.

72. **The area of a DNA nucleotide that varies is the... (Skill 2.1)(Rigorous)**

    A. deoxyribose.
    B. phosphate group.
    C. nitrogenous base.
    D. sugar.

73. **A DNA strand has the base sequence of TCAGTA. Its DNA complement would have the following sequence. (Skill 2.1)(Moderate Rigor)**

    A. ATGACT
    B. TCAGTA
    C. AGUCAU
    D. AGTCAT

74. **Genes function in specifying the structure of which molecule? (Skill 2.1)(Rigorous)**

    A. carbohydrates
    B. lipids
    C. nucleic acids
    D. proteins

75. **What is the correct order of steps in protein synthesis? (Skill 2.1)(Moderate Rigor)**

    A. transcription, then replication
    B. transcription, then translation
    C. translation, then transcription
    D. replication, then translation

76. **This carries amino acids to the ribosome in protein synthesis. (Skill 2.1) (Easy Rigor)**

    A. messenger RNA
    B. ribosomal RNA
    C. transfer RNA
    D. DNA

77. **A protein is sixty amino acids in length. This requires a coded DNA sequence of how many nucleotides? (Skill 2.1) (Rigorous)**

    A. 20
    B. 30
    C. 120
    D. 180

78. **A DNA molecule has the sequence of ACTATG. What is the anticodon of this molecule? (Skill 2.1)(Moderate Rigor)**

    A. UGAUAC
    B. ACUAUG
    C. TGATAC
    D. ACTATG

79. **Any change that affects the sequence of bases in a gene is called a(n)...(Skill 2.1)(Rigorous)**

    A. deletion.
    B. polyploid.
    C. mutation.
    D. duplication.

80. **Segments of DNA can be transferred from the DNA of one organism to another through the use of which of the following? (Skill 2.1)(Moderate Rigor)**

    A. bacterial plasmids
    B. viruses
    C. chromosomes from frogs
    D. plant DNA

81. **The quaternary structure of proteins is: (Skill 2.1)(Rigorous)**

    A. The overall structure of the protein from the aggregation of two or more polypeptide chains.

    B. formed by bonding between the side chains of the amino acids

    C. the coils and folds of polypeptide chains

    D. the protein's unique sequence of amino acids

82. **The enzyme that unwinds DNA during replication is: (Skill 2.1)(Moderate Rigor)**

    A. DNAse

    B. replicase

    C. helicase

    D. topoisomerases

83. **A small circular piece of DNA that contains accessory DNA is called:(Skill 2.1)(Moderate Rigor)**

    A. mitochondrial DNA

    B. messenger RNA

    C. transfer DNA

    D. plasmid

84. **The order of DNA duplication is the following: (Skill 2.1)(Moderate Rigor)**

    A. termination, elongation, initiation

    B. initiation, elongation, termination

    C. elongation, initiation, termination

    D. initiation, termination, elongation

85. In DNA, adenine bonds with _____, while cytosine bonds with _____. (Skill 2.1)(Moderate Rigor)

   A. thymine/guanine
   B. adenine/cytosine
   C. cytosine/adenine
   D. guanine/thymine

86. Which protein structure consists of the coils and folds of polypeptide chains? (Skill 2.1)(Moderate Rigor)

   A. secondary structure
   B. quaternary structure
   C. tertiary structure
   D. primary structure

87. Homozygous individuals...(Skill 2.2)(Easy Rigor)

   A. have two different alleles.
   B. are of the same species.
   C. have the same features.
   D. have a pair of identical alleles.

88. The term "phenotype" refers to which of the following? (Skill 2.2)(Moderate Rigor)

   A. a condition which is heterozygous
   B. the genetic makeup of an individual
   C. a condition which is homozygous
   D. how the genotype is expressed

89. The ratio of brown-eyed to blue-eyed children from the mating of a blue-eyed male to a heterozygous brown-eyed female is expected to be which of the following? (Skill 2.2)(Moderate Rigor)

   A. 2:1
   B. 1:1
   C. 1:0
   D. 1:2

90. The Law of Segregation defined by Mendel states that...(Skill 2.2)(Moderate Rigor)

   A. when sex cells form, the two alleles that determine a trait will end up on different gametes.
   B. only one of two alleles is expressed in a heterozygous organism.
   C. the allele expressed is the dominant allele.
   D. alleles of one trait do not affect the inheritance of alleles on another chromosome.

91. When a white flower is crossed with a red flower, incomplete dominance can be seen by the production of which of the following?(Skill 2.2)(Easy Rigor)

   A. pink flowers
   B. red flowers
   C. white flowers
   D. red and white flowers

92. **A child with type O blood has a father with type A blood and a mother with type B blood. The genotypes of the parents respectively would be which of the following? (Skill 2.2)(Easy Rigor)**

    A. AA and BO
    B. AO and BO
    C. AA and BB
    D. AO and OO

93. **Crossing over, which increases genetic diversity occurs during which stage(s)? (Skill 2.2)(Rigorous)**

    A. telophase II in meiosis
    B. metaphase in mitosis
    C. interphase in both mitosis and meiosis
    D. prophase I in meiosis

94. **The type of allele dominance found in ABO blood grouping is: (Skill 2.2)(Moderate Rigor)**

    A. Autosomal dominance

    B. Incomplete dominance

    C. Codominance

    D. Complete dominance

95. **In a punnet square with a single trait, what are the ratios of genotypes produced? (Skill 2.2)(Moderate Rigor)**

    A. 1:2:2

    B. 2:1:1

    C. 1:1:1

    D. 1:2:1

96. **The organism's genetic makeup is called: (Skill 2.2)(Moderate Rigor)**

    A. Heterozygote

    B. Genotype

    C. Phenotype

    D. Homozygote

97. **The law that states that only one of the two possible alleles from each parent is passed on to the offspring is called: (Skill 2.2)(Moderate Rigor)**

    A. The Mendelian Law

    B. The Law of independent assortment

    C. The law of segregation

    D. The allele law

98. **The *lac* operon (Skill 2.3)(Rigorous)**

    I. contains the *lac Z, lac Y,* and *lac A* genes
    II. converts glucose to lactose
    III. contains a repressor
    IV. is on when the repressor is activated

    A. I
    B. II
    C. III and IV
    D. I and III

99. A genetic engineering advancement in the medical field is... (Skill 2.4)(Easy Rigor)

   A. gene therapy.
   B. pesticides.
   C. degradation of harmful chemicals.
   D. antibiotics.

100. Which of the following is not true regarding restriction enzymes?(Skill 2.4)(Moderate Rigor)

   A. they aid in transcombination procedures
   B. they are used in genetic engineering
   C. they are named after the bacteria in which they naturally occur
   D. they identify and splice certain base sequences on DNA

101. What is not one of the modern uses of DNA? (Skill 2.4)(Moderate Rigor)

   A. PCR technology

   B. Gene therapy

   C. Cloning

   D. Genetic Alignment

102. Gel electrophoresis: (Skill 2.4)(Rigorous)

   A. isolates fragments of DNA for scientific purposes

   B. cannot be used in proteins

   C. requires the polymerase chain reaction

   D. only separates DNA by size

103. The duplication of genetic material into another cell is called: (Skill 2.4)(Moderate Rigor)

   A. replicating

   B. cell duplication

   C. cloning

   D. genetic restructuring

104. Electrophoresis separates DNA on the basis of... (Skill 2.4)(Rigorous)

   A. amount of current.
   B. molecular size.
   C. positive charge of the molecule.
   D. solubility of the gel.

105. Reproductive isolation results in... (Skill 3.1)(Moderate Rigor)

   A. extinction.
   B. migration.
   C. follilization.
   D. speciation.

106. What is true about natural selection? (Skill 3.1)(Moderate Rigor)

A. It acts on an individual genotype

B. It does not happen currently

C. It is a phenomenon of animals only

D. It acts on the individual phenotype

107. How does diversity aid a population? (Skill 3.1)(Rigorous)

A. It provides possible improvements to the population.

B. Mates are attracted to a diverse population.

C. Potential mates like conformity.

D. It increases the DNA differences in the population.

108. DNA synthesis results in a strand that is synthesized continuously. This is the... (Skill 3.1)(Rigorous)

A. lagging strand.
B. leading strand.
C. template strand.
D. complementary strand.

109. What is not true of diversity? (Skill 3.2)(Moderate Rigor)

A. Without diversity there would be extinction.

B. Diversity is increasing all the time.

C. Fossil evidence supports diversity.

D. Skeletons are too similar to allow for diversity.

110. Darwin supported the evolutionary Theory of: (Skill 3.2)(Rigorous)

A. Punctualism

B. Gradualism

C. Equilibrium

D. Convergency

111. What is not true about reproductive isolation? (Skill 3.2)(Moderate Rigor)

A. It prevents populations from exchanging genes

B. It can occur by preventing fertilization.

C. It can result in speciation

D. It is not a phenomenon of islands

112. **Members of the same species...**
     (Skill 3.2)(Easy Rigor)

     A. look identical.
     B. never change.
     C. reproduce successfully within their group.
     D. live in the same geographic location.

113. **Which of the following factors will affect the Hardy-Weinberg law of equilibrium, leading to evolutionary change?(Skill 3.2) (Moderate Rigor)**

     A. no mutations
     B. non-random mating
     C. no immigration or emigration
     D. large population

114. **If a population is in Hardy-Weinberg equilibrium and the frequency of the recessive allele is .3, what percentage of the population is expected to be heterozygous? (Skill 3.2)(Rigorous)**

     A. 9%
     B. 49%
     C. 42%
     D. 21%

115. **Which aspect of science does not support evolution? (Skill 3.2)(Moderate Rigor)**

     A. comparative anatomy
     B. organic chemistry
     C. comparison of DNA among organisms
     D. analogous structures

116. **Evolution occurs in...**
     (Skill 3.2)(Easy Rigor)

     A. individuals.
     B. populations.
     C. organ systems.
     D. cells.

117. **Which process contributes most to the large variety of living things in the world today? (Skill 3.2)(Moderate Rigor)**

     A. meiosis
     B. asexual reproduction
     C. mitosis
     D. alternation of generations

118. **All of the following gases made up the primitive atmosphere except... (Skill 3.4)(Moderate Rigor)**

     A. ammonia.
     B. methane.
     C. oxygen.
     D. hydrogen.

119. **The Endosymbiotic Theory states that... (Skill 3.4)(Rigorous)**

     A. eukaryotes arose from prokaryotes.
     B. animals evolved in close r relationships with one another.
     C. the prokaryotes arose from eukaryotes.
     D. life arose from inorganic compounds.

120. The wing of a bird, human arm, and whale flipper have the same bone structure. These are called...
(Skill 3.3)(Moderate Rigor)

A. polymorphic structures.
B. homologous structures.
C. vestigial structures.
D. analogous structures.

121. Which of the following is not an abiotic factor?
(Skill 3.4)(Moderate Rigor)

A. temperature
B. rainfall
C. soil quality
D. bacteria

122. Which was not a stage in the origin of life? (Skill 3.4)(Moderate Rigor)

A. Abiotic

B. Biotic

C. Formation of polymers

D. Accumulation of probionts

123. What is not true about Cladistics? (Skill 3.4)(Rigorous)

A. It is the study of phylogenetic relationships of organisms

B. It involves a branching diagram that uses the development of novel traits to separate groups of organisms.

C. It distinguishes between the relative importance of the traits.

D. It shows when traits developed with respect to other traits.

124. If DDT were present in an ecosystem, which of the following organisms would have the highest concentration in its system?
(Skill 4.1)(Rigorous)

A. grasshopper

B. eagle

C. frog

D. crabgrass

125. What eats secondary consumers? (Skill 4.2)(Moderate Rigor)

A. Producers

B. Tertiary consumers

C. Primary consumers

D. Decomposers

126. **What is true of the water cycle? (Skill 4.2)(Moderate Rigor)**

   A. Two percent of the water is fixed and unavailable.

   B. 75% of available water is groundwater.

   C. The water cycle is driven by the ocean currents.

   D. Surface water is unavailable.

127. **What is not true of the carbon cycle? (Skill 4.2)(Moderate Rigor)**

   A. Ten percent of all available carbon is in the air.

   B. Carbon dioxide is fixed by glycosylation.

   C. Plants fix carbon in the form of glucose.

   D. Animals release carbon through respiration.

128. **Sulfur oxides and nitrogen oxides in the environment react with water to cause... (Skill 4.2)(Moderate Rigor)**

   A. ammonia.
   B. acidic precipitation.
   C. sulfuric acid.
   D. global warming.

129. **In the comparison of respiration**

to photosynthesis, which statement is true?(Skill 4.2)(Rigorous)

   A. oxygen is a waste product in photosynthesis but not in respiration

   B. glucose is produced in respiration but not in photosynthesis

   C. carbon dioxide is formed in photosynthesis but not in respiration

   D. water is formed in respiration but not in photosynthesis

130. **Which term is not associated with the water cycle? (Skill 4.2)(Moderate Rigor)**

   A. precipitation
   B. transpiration
   C. fixation
   D. evaporation

131. All of the following are density independent factors that affect a population except...
(Skill 4.2)(Easy Rigor)

A. temperature.
B. rainfall.
C. predation.
D. soil nutrients.

132. High humidity and temperature stability are present in which of the following biomes?
(Skill 4.2)(Easy Rigor)

A. taiga
B. deciduous forest
C. desert
D. tropical rain forest

133. Which trophic level has the highest ecological efficiency?
(Skill 4.2)(Moderate Rigor)

A. decomposers
B. producers
C. tertiary consumers
D. secondary consumers

134. Oxygen created in photosynthesis comes from the breakdown of... (Skill 4.2)(Easy Rigor)

A. carbon dioxide.
B. water.
C. glucose.
D. carbon monoxide.

135. What is not true of decomposers? (Skill 4.2)(Rigorous)

A. Decomposers recycle the carbon accumulated in durable organic material

B. Ammonification is the decomposition of organic nitrogen back to ammonia.

C. Decomposers add phosphorous back to the soil

D. Decomposers belong to the Genus Escherichia.

136. A virus that can remain dormant until a certain environmental condition causes its rapid increase is said to be...
(Skill 4.3)(Moderate Rigor)

A. lytic.
B. benign.
C. saprophytic.
D. lysogenic.

137. A clownfish is protected by the sea anemone's tentacles. In turn, the anemone receives uneaten food from the clownfish. This is an example of... (Skill 4.3)(Easy Rigor)

A. mutualism.
B. parasitism.
C. commensalism.
D. competition.

138. Which of the following does not result in the detriment of one species and the advancement of another? (Skill 4.3)(Moderate Rigor)

A. Parasitism

B. Mutualism

C. Predation

D. Herbivory

139. In an experiment measuring the growth of bacteria at different temperatures, identify the independent variable. (Skill 5.2)(Moderate Rigor)

A. growth of number of colonies
B. temperature
C. type of bacteria used
D. light intensity

140. Primary succession occurs after...
(Skill 5.3)(Moderate Rigor)

A. nutrient enrichment.
B. a forest fire.
C. bare rock is exposed after a water table recedes.
D. a housing development is built.

141. A scientific theory...(Skill 6.1)(Moderate Rigor)

A. proves scientific accuracy.
B. is never rejected.
C. results in a medical breakthrough.
D. may be altered at a later time.

142. Which is the correct order of methodology? 1) testing revised explanation, 2) setting up a controlled experiment to test an explanation, 3) drawing a conclusion, 4) suggesting an explanation for observations, and 5) comparing observed results to hypothesized results(Skill 6.1)(Rigorous)

A. 4, 2, 3, 1, 5
B. 3, 1, 4, 2, 5
C. 4, 2, 5, 1, 3
D. 2, 5, 4, 1, 3

143. Given a choice, which is the most desirable method of heating a substance in the lab? (Skill 7.4) (Easy Rigor)

A. alcohol burner
B. gas burner
C. bunsen burner
D. hot plate

144. Biological waste should be disposed of... (Skill 7.4)(Easy Rigor)

A. in the trash can.
B. under a fume hood.
C. in the broken glass box.
D. in an autoclavable biohazard bag.

145. Chemicals should be stored...(Skill 7.4)(Easy Rigor)

A. in a cool dark room.
B. in a dark room.
C. according to their reactivity with other substances.
D. in a double locked room.

146. Who should be notified in the case of a serious chemical spill? (Skill 7.4)(Moderate Rigor)

   I.   the custodian
   II. the fire department
   III. the chemistry teacher
   IV. the administration

   A. I
   B. II
   C. II and III
   D. II and IV

147. The "Right to Know" law states...(Skill 7.4)(Rigorous)

   A. the inventory of toxic chemicals checked against the "Substance List" be available.
   B. that students are to be informed of alternatives to dissection.
   C. that science teachers are to be informed of student allergies.
   D. that students are to be informed of infectious microorganisms used in lab.

148. In which situation would a science teacher be liable? (Skill 7.4)(Moderate Rigor)

   A. a teacher leaves to receive an emergency phone call and a student slips and falls
   B. a student removes their goggles and gets dissection fluid in their eye
   C. a faulty gas line results in a fire
   D. a student cuts himself with a scalpel

149. Which statement best defines negligence? (Skill 7.4)(Easy Rigor)

   A. failure to give oral instructions for those with reading disabilities
   B. failure to exercise ordinary care
   C. inability to supervise a large group of students
   D. reasonable anticipation that an event may occur

150. Which item should always be used when using chemicals with noxious vapors? (Skill 7.4)(Easy Rigor)

   A. eye protection
   B. face shield
   C. fume hood
   D. lab apron

Answer Key

1. C	39. C	77. D	115. B
2. D	40. A	78. B	116. B
3. A	41. A	79. C	117. A
4. A	42. C	80. A	118. C
5. D	43. C	81. A	119. A
6. C	44. C	82. C	120. B
7. A	45. A	83. D	121. D
8. B	46. D	84. B	122. B
9. A	47. C	85. A	123. C
10. B	48. A	86. A	124. B
11. D	49. B	87. D	125. B
12. D	50. D	88. D	126. A
13. A	51. C	89. B	127. B
14. C	52. A	90. A	128. B
15. A	53. B	91. A	129. A
16. D	54. A	92. B	130. C
17. D	55. B	93. D	131. C
18. A	56. A	94. C	132. D
19. A	57. D	95. D	133. B
20. D	58. B	96. B	134. B
21. D	59. A	97. B	135. D
22. B	60. A	98. D	136. D
23. C	61. A	99. A	137. A
24. B	62. D	100. A	138. B
25. B	63. C	101. D	139. B
26. B	64. B	102. A	140. C
27. C	65. D	103. C	141. D
28. A	66. C	104. B	142. C
29. D	67. C	105. D	143. D
30. D	68. A	106. D	144. D
31. B	69. B	107. A	145. C
32. C	70. C	108. B	146. D
33. A	71. B	109. D	147. A
34. C	72. C	110. B	148. A
35. C	73. D	111. D	149. B
36. B	74. D	112. C	150. C
37. D	75. B	113. B	
38. D	76. C	114. C	

Rigor Table

Easy Rigor 20%	Moderate Rigor 60%	Rigorous 20%
4, 7, 15, 36, 37, 40, 46, 52, 54, 57, 60, 61, 63, 66, 76, 87, 91, 92, 99, 112, 116, 131, 132, 134, 137, 143, 144, 145, 149, 150	1, 2, 3, 5, 6, 8, 9, 10, 12, 13, 16, 17,18, 19, 20, 22, 23, 24, 25, 26, 27, 28, 29, 30, 31, 32, 34, 35, 38, 39, 42, 43, 44, 45, 47, 48, 49, 51, 53, 55, 58, 62, 64, 65, 68, 69, 71, 73, 75, 78, 80, 82, 83, 84, 85, 86, 88, 89, 90, 94,95,96,97,100,101, 103, 105, 106, 109, 111, 113, 115, 117, 118, 120, 121, 122, 125, 126, 127 ,128, 130, 133, 136, 138, 139, 140, 141, 146, 148	11, 14, 21, 33, 41, 50, 56, 59, 67, 70, 72, 74, 77, 79, 81, 93, 98, 102, 104, 107, 108, 110, 114, 119, 123, 124, 129, 135, 142,147

Rationales with Sample Questions

1.   **Which is not true about a cell membrane? (Skill 1.1)(Moderate Rigor)**

    A. It is made from phospholipids
    B. Both plant and animal cells have a cell membrane.
    C. The cell wall is the same as the cell membrane in plants.
    D. It controls the passage of nutrients within a cell.

C. The cell wall is the same as the cell membrane in plants
Both plants and animals have cell membranes but plant cells also have an outer cell wall to give it structure.

2.   **Microorganisms use all but the following to move: (Skill 1.1)(Moderate Rigor)**

    A. Pseudopods
    B. Flagella
    C. Cilia
    D. Pili

D. Pseudopods
Pseudopods, flagella and cilia are used by microorganisms for movement. Pili are used for attachment.

3.   **Eukaryotic cells are found in all but the following:(Skill 1.1)(Moderate Rigor)**

    A. Bacteria
    B. Protists
    C. Fungi
    D. Animals

A. Bacteria
Eukaryotic cells are found in protists, fungi, plants and animals but not in bacteria.

4.   **Which kingdom is comprised of organisms made of one cell with no nuclear membrane? (Skill 1.1)(Easy Rigor)**

      A.   Monera
      B.   Protista
      C.   Fungi
      D.   Algae

A. Monera
Monera is the only kingdom that is made up of unicellular organisms with no nucleus. Algae is a protist because it is made up of one type of tissue and it has a nucleus.

5.   **Rough endoplasmic reticulum contains: (Skill 1.1)(Moderate Rigor)**

      A. Vacuoles
      B. Mitochondria
      C. Microfilaments
      D. Ribosomes

D. Ribosomes
Rough endoplasmic reticulum is defined as such because of the occurrence of ribosomes on its surface.

6.   **Identify the correct sequence of organization of living things. (Skill 1.1)(Moderate Rigor)**

      A. cell – organelle – organ system – tissue – organ – organism
      B. cell – tissue – organ – organ system – organelle – organism
      C. organelle – cell – tissue – organ – organ system – organism
      D. tissue – organelle – organ – cell – organism – organ system

C. organelle – cell – tissue – organ – organ system - organism
An organism, such as a human, is comprised of several organ systems such as the circulatory and nervous systems. These organ systems consist of many organs including the heart and the brain. These organs are made of tissue such as cardiac muscle. Tissues are made up of cells, which contain organelles like the mitochondria and the Golgi apparatus.

7.   **Which is not a characteristic of living things? (Skill 1.1)(Easy Rigor)**

    A. movement
    B. cellular structure
    C. metabolism
    D. reproduction

A. movement
Movement is not a characteristic of life. Viruses are considered non-living organisms but have the ability to move from cell to cell in its host organism. A leaf on a tree or the tree itself are very much alive but unable to move in terms of mobility.

8.   **The purpose of the Golgi Apparatus is: (Skill 1.1)(Moderate Rigor)**

    A. To break down proteins
    B. To sort, modify and package molecules
    C. To break down fats
    D. To make carbohydrates.

B. To sort, modify and package molecules
The Golgi Apparatus takes molecules from the endoplasmic reticulum and sorts, modifies and packages the molecules for later use by the cell.

9.   **The amyloplasts: (Skill 1.1)(Moderate Rigor)**

    A. Store starch in a plant cell
    B. Store waste in animal cells
    C. Store green and yellow pigment
    D. Aid in photosynthesis.

A. Store starch in a plant cell. Amyloplasts store starch in plant cells

10. **The largest of the three fibers found in cells are called: (Skill 1.1)(Moderate Rigor)**

    A. Intermediate filaments
    B. Microtubules
    C. Microfilaments
    D. Filaments

B. Microtubules
The order of size of filaments from smallest to largest are microfilaments, intermediate filaments and microtubules.

11.   **The Archaea organisms are all but the following: (Skill 1.1)(Rigorous)**

   A. Methanogens
   B. Halobacteria
   C. Thermaoacidophiles
   D. Bacteriophiles

D.   Bacteriophiles
The Archaea group includes all of the above except Bacteriophiles.

12.   **The first cells that evolved on earth were probably of which type? (Skill 1.1)(Moderate Rigor)**

   A. autotrophs
   B. eukaryotes
   C. heterotrophs
   D. prokaryotes

D. prokaryotes
Prokaryotes date back to 3.5 billion years ago in the first fossil record. Their ability to adapt to the environment allows them to thrive in a wide variety of habitats.

13.   **Oxygen is given off in the... (Skill 1.1)(Moderate Rigor)**

   A. light reactions of photosynthesis.
   B. dark reactions of photosynthesis.
   C. Krebs cycle.
   D. reduction of NAD+ to NADH.

A. light reactions of photosynthesis
The conversion of solar energy to chemical energy occurs in the light reactions. Electrons are transferred by the absorption of light by chlorophyll and cause water to split, releasing oxygen as a waste product.

14.   Bacteria commonly reproduce by a process called binary fission. Which of the following best defines this process? (Skill 1.1)(Rigorous)

      A. viral vectors carry DNA to new bacteria
      B. DNA from one bacterium enters another
      C. DNA doubles and the bacterial cell divides
      D. DNA from dead cells is absorbed into bacteria

C. DNA doubles and the bacterial cell divides
Binary fission is the asexual process in which the bacteria divide in half after the DNA doubles. This results in an exact clone of the parent cell.

15.   The shape of a cell depends on its... (Skill 1.1)(Easy Rigor)

      A. function.
      B. structure.
      C. age.
      D. size.

A. function
In most living organisms, cellular shape depends upon the cell's structure which is based on its function.

16.   The individual parts of cells are best studied using a(n)... (Skill 1.1)(Moderate Rigor)

      A. ultracentrifuge.
      B. phase-contrast microscope.
      C. CAT scan.
      D. electron microscope.

D. electron microscope
The scanning electron microscope uses a beam of electrons to pass through the specimen. The resolution is about 1000 times greater than that of a light microscope. This allows the scientist to view extremely small objects, such as the individual parts of a cell.

17.   **Thermoacidophiles are... (Skill 1.1)(Moderate Rigor)**

A. prokaryotes.
B. eukaryotes.
C. protists.
D. archaea.

D. archaea
Thermoacidophiles, methanogens, and halobacteria are members of the archaea group.

18.   **Which of the following is not a type of fiber that makes up the cytoskeleton? (Skill 1.1)(Moderate Rigor)**

A. vacuoles
B. microfilaments
C. microtubules
D. intermediate filaments

A. vacuoles
Vacuoles are mostly found in plants and hold stored food and pigments. The other three choices are fibers that make up the cytoskeleton found in both plant and animal cells.

19.   **Viruses are made of... (Skill 1.1)(Moderate Rigor)**

A. a protein coat surrounding a nucleic acid.
B. DNA, RNA, and a cell wall.
C. a nucleic acid surrounding a protein coat.
D. protein surrounded by DNA.

A. a protein coat surrounding a nucleic acid.
Viruses are composed of a protein coat surrounding a nucleic acid; either RNA or DNA.

20.   **Protists are classified into major groups according to... (Skill 1.1)(Moderate Rigor)**

        A. their method of obtaining nutrition.
        B. reproduction.
        C. metabolism.
        D. their form and function.

D. their form and function
The chaotic status of names and concepts of the higher classification of the protists reflects their great diversity in form, function, and life styles. The protists are often grouped as algae (plant-like), protozoa (animal-like), or fungus-like based on the similarity of their lifestyle and characteristics to these more defined groups.

21.   **This stage of mitosis includes cytokinesis or division of the cytoplasm and its organelles. (Skill 1.2)(Rigorous)**

        A. anaphase
        B. interphase
        C. prophase
        D. telophase

D. telophase
The last stage of the mitotic phase is telophase. Here, the two nuclei form with a full set of DNA each. The cell is pinched into two cells and cytokinesis, or division of the cytoplasm and organelles, occurs.

22.   **Replication of chromosomes occurs during which phase of the cell cycle? (Skill 1.2)(Moderate Rigor)**

        A. prophase
        B. interphase
        C. metaphase
        D. anaphase

B. interphase
Interphase is the stage where the cell grows and copies the chromosomes in preparation for the mitotic phase.

23.   **Which statement regarding mitosis is correct? (Skill 1.2)(Moderate Rigor)**

        A. diploid cells produce haploid cells for sexual reproduction
        B. sperm and egg cells are produced
        C. diploid cells produce diploid cells for growth and repair
        D. it allows for greater genetic diversity

C. diploid cells produce diploid cells for growth and repair
The purpose of mitotic cell division is to provide growth and repair in body (somatic) cells. The cells begin as diploid and produce diploid cells.

24.   **In a plant cell, telophase is described as... (Skill 1.2)(Moderate Rigor)**

        A. the time of chromosome doubling.
        B. cell plate formation.
        C. the time when crossing over occurs.
        D. cleavage furrow formation.

B. cell plate formation
During plant cell telophase, a cell plate is observed whereas a cleavage furrow is formed in animal cells.

25.   **Identify this stage of mitosis. (Skill 1.2)(Moderate Rigor)**

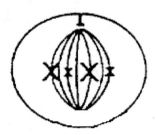

        A. anaphase
        B. metaphase
        C. telophase
        D. prophase

B. metaphase
During metaphase, the centromeres are at opposite ends of the cell. Here the chromosomes are aligned with one another.

26. **Identify this stage of mitosis. (Skill 1.2)(Moderate Rigor)**

   A. prophase
   B. telophase
   C. anaphase
   D. metaphase

B. telophase
Telophase is the last stage of mitosis. Here, two nuclei become visible and the nuclear membrane reassembles.

27. **Which process(es) result(s) in a haploid chromosome number? (Skill 1.2)(Moderate Rigor)**

   A. both meiosis and mitosis
   B. mitosis
   C. meiosis
   D. replication and division

C. meiosis
In meiosis, there are two consecutive cell divisions resulting in the reduction of the chromosome number by half (diploid to haploid).

28. **Identify this stage of mitosis. (Skill 1.2)(Moderate Rigor)**

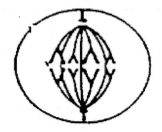

A. anaphase
B. metaphase
C. prophase
D. telophase

A. anaphase
During anaphase, the centromeres split in half and homologous chromosomes separate.

29. **Which of the following is a monomer? (Skill 1.3)(Moderate Rigor)**

A. RNA
B. glycogen
C. DNA
D. amino acid

D. amino acid
A monomer is the simplest unit of structure for a particular macromolecule. Amino acids are the basic units that comprise a protein. RNA and DNA are polymers consisting of nucleotides and glycogen is a polymer consisting of many molecules of glucose.

30. **Which does not affect enzyme rate? (Skill 1.3)(Moderate Rigor)**

    A. increase of temperature
    B. amount of substrate
    C. pH
    D. size of the cell

D. size of the cell
Temperature and pH can affect the rate of reaction of an enzyme. The amount of substrate affects the enzyme as well. The enzyme acts on the substrate. The more substrate, the slower the enzyme rate. Therefore, the only choice left is D, the size of the cell, which has no effect on enzyme rate.

31. **All but which one of the following are true of a cell membrane: (Skill 1.3) (Moderate Rigor)**

    A. It contains polar and nonpolar phospholipids
    B. It only uses active transport to transport molecules across the membrane.
    C. It contains cholesterol
    D. It has proteins imbedded in it.

B. It only uses active transplort to transplort molecules across the membrane
Cell membranes use passive and active transport to transport molecules across the membrane.

32. **Facilitated diffusion: (Skill 1.3)(Moderate Rigor)**

    A. Requires energy
    B. Only happens in plant cells
    C. Requires a transport molecule to pass through the membrane.
    D. Only allows molecules to leave a cell but not to enter it.

C. Requires a transport molecule to pass through the membrane
Facilitated diffusion requires no energy but needs a transport molecule to pass another molecule through the membrane.

33. **The fluidity of the cell membrane is determined by: (Skill 1.3)(Rigorous)**

    A. Cholesterol
    B. Phospholipids
    C. Imbedded Proteins
    D. DNA

A. Cholesterol
It is the cholesterol in the cell membranes that determines its fluidity.

34. **What is not true of enzymes? (Skill 1.3)(Moderate Rigor)**

    A. They are the most diverse of all proteins.
    B. They act on a substrate.
    C. They work at a wide range of pH.
    D. They are temperature-dependent.

C. They work at a wide range of pH
Enzymes generally work best within a very narrow range in pH.

35. **What is necessary for diffusion to occur? (Skill 1.3)(Moderate Rigor)**

    A. carrier proteins
    B. energy
    C. a concentration gradient
    D. a membrane

C. a concentration gradient
Diffusion is the ability of molecules to move from areas of high concentration to areas of low concentration (a concentration gradient).

36.   **Which is an example of the use of energy to move a substance through a membrane from areas of low concentration to areas of high concentration? (Skill 1.3)(Easy Rigor)**

        A. osmosis
        B. active transport
        C. exocytosis
        D. phagocytosis

B. active transport
Active transport can move substances with or against the concentration gradient. This energy-requiring process allows for molecules to move from areas of low concentration to areas of high concentration.

37. **A plant cell is placed in salt water. The resulting movement of water out of the cell is called... (Skill 1.3)(Easy Rigor)**

        A. facilitated diffusion.
        B. diffusion.
        C. transpiration.
        D. osmosis.

D. osmosis
Osmosis is simply the diffusion of water across a semi-permeable membrane. Water will diffuse out of the cell if there is a lower concentration of water on the outside of the cell.

38.   **What are the monomers in polysaccharides? (Skill 1.3)(Moderate rigor)**

        A. Nucleotides
        B. Amino acids
        C. Polypeptides
        D. Simple sugars

D. Simple sugars
The monomers of polysaccharides are simple sugars.

39.   A type of molecule not found in the membrane of an animal cell is...
       (Skill 1.3)(Moderate Rigor)

       A. phospholipid.
       B. protein.
       C. cellulose.
       D. cholesterol.

C. cellulose
Phospholipids, protein, and cholesterol are all found in animal cells. Cellulose, however, is only found in plant cells.

40.   Which type of cell would contain the most mitochondria? (Skill
       1.3)(Easy Rigor)

       A. muscle cell
       B. nerve cell
       C. epithelium
       D. blood cell

A. muscle cell
Mitochondria are the site of cellular respiration where ATP is made. Muscle cells have the most mitochondria because they use a great deal of energy.

41.   According to the fluid-mosaic model of the cell membrane,
       membranes are composed of... (Skill 1.3)(Rigorous)

       A. phospholipid bilayers with proteins embedded in the layers.
       B. one layer of phospholipids with cholesterol embedded in the layer.
       C. two layers of protein with lipids embedded the layers.
       D. DNA and fluid proteins.

A. phospholipid bilayers with proteins embedded in the layers
Cell membranes are composed of two phospholipids with their hydrophobic tails sandwiched between their hydrophilic heads, creating a lipid bilayer. The membrane contains proteins embedded in the layer (integral proteins) and proteins on the surface (peripheral proteins).

42. All the following statements regarding both a mitochondria and a
     chloroplast are correct except... (Skill 1.3)(Moderate Rigor)

     A. they both produce energy over a gradient.
     B. they both have DNA and are capable of reproduction.
     C. they both transform light energy to chemical energy.
     D. they both make ATP.

C. they both transform light energy to chemical energy
Cellular respiration does not transform light energy to chemical energy. Cellular
respiration transfers electrons to release energy. Photosynthesis utilizes light
energy to produce chemical energy.

43. Which is the correct statement regarding the human nervous system
     and the human endocrine system? (Skill 1.3)(Moderate Rigor)

     A. the nervous system maintains homeostasis whereas the endocrine
         system does not
     B. endocrine glands produce neurotransmitters whereas nerves produce
         hormones
     C. nerve signals travel on neurons whereas hormones travel through the
         blood
     D. the nervous system involves chemical transmission whereas the
         endocrine system does not

C. nerve signals travel on neurons whereas hormones travel through the blood
In the human nervous system, neurons carry nerve signals to and from the cell
body. Endocrine glands produce hormones that are carried through the body in
the bloodstream.

44. The most ATP is generated through... (Skill 1.3)(Moderate Rigor)

     A. fermentation.
     B. glycolysis.
     C. chemiosmosis.
     D. the Krebs cycle.

C. chemiosmosis
The electron transport chain uses electrons to pump hydrogen ions across
the mitochondrial membrane. This ion gradient is used to form ATP in a process
called chemiosmosis. ATP is generated by the removal of hydrogen ions from
NADH and $FADH_2$. This yields 34 ATP molecules.

45. The function of the cardiovascular system is to: (Skill 1.4) (Moderate Rigor)

   A. Move oxygenated blood around the body via a pump and tubes
   B. To oxygenate the blood through gas exchange.
   C. To act as an exocrine system
   D. To flush toxins out of the body

A. Move oxygenated blood around the body via a pump and tubes
The cardiovascular system moves oxygenated blood around the body via the heart (a pump) and tubes (arteries and veins)

46. Parts of the nervous system include all but the following: (Skill 1.4) (Easy Rigor)

   A. brain
   B. spinal cord
   C. axons
   D. venules

D. venules
Venules are part of the circulatory system. The others are part of the nervous system.

47. Homeostatic mechanisms in the body include all but the following: (Skill 1.4) (Moderate Rigor)

   A. Thermoregulation
   B. Excretion
   C. Respiration
   D. Osmoregulation

C. Respiration
All but respiration are homeostatic mechanisms used by the body to achieve homeostasis.

48. The body's endocrine mechanisms are controlled by: (Skill 1.4) (Moderate Rigor)

   A. Feedback loops
   B. Control molecules
   C. Neurochemicals
   D. Neurotransmitters

A. Feedback loops

The body's mechanisms are controlled by feedback loops.

49. **The gland that regulated the calcium in the body is the: (Skill 1.4) (Moderate Rigor)**

A. Thyroid gland
B. Parathyroid gland
C. Hypothalamus
D. Pituitary gland

B. Parathyroid gland
The parathyroid glands regulate the calcium levels in the body. They are imbedded within the thyroid gland.

50. **What is not one of the three gonadal steroids? (Skill 1.4)(Rigorous)**

A. Testosterone
B. Estrogen
C. Progesterone
D. ACTH

D. ACTH
ACTH is not one of the three steroids produced by the gonads. The other three are made by the gonads.

51. **The most common neurotransmitter is: (Skill 1.4)(Moderate Rigor)**

A. epinephrine
B. serotonin
C. Acetyl choline
D. norepinephrine

C. Acetyl choline
The most common neurotransmitter is acetyl choline.

52. **Food is carried through the digestive tract by a series of wave-like contractions. This process is called... (Skill 1.4)(Easy Rigor)**

    A. peristalsis.
    B. chyme.
    C. digestion.
    D. absorption.

A. peristalsis
Peristalsis is the process of wave-like contractions that moves food through the digestive tract.

53. **Movement is possible by the action of muscles pulling on... (Skill 1.4)(Moderate Rigor)**

    A. skin.
    B. bones.
    C. joints.
    D. ligaments.

B. bones
The muscular system's function is for movement. Skeletal muscles are attached to bones and are responsible for their movement.

54. **All of the following are functions of the skin except... (Skill 1.4)(Easy Rigor)**

    A. storage.
    B. protection.
    C. sensation.
    D. regulation of temperature.

A. storage
Skin is a protective barrier against infection. It contains hair follicles that respond to sensation and it plays a role in thermoregulation.

55.   Hormones are essential to the regulation of reproduction. What organ is responsible for the release of hormones for sexual maturity? (Skill 1.4)(Moderate Rigor)

A. pituitary gland
B. hypothalamus
C. pancreas
D. thyroid gland

B. hypothalamus
The hypothalamus begins secreting hormones that help mature the reproductive system and stimulate development of the secondary sex characteristics.

56.   A bicyclist has a heart rate of 110 beats per minute and a stroke volume of 85 mL per beat. What is the cardiac output? (Skill 1.4)(Rigorous)

A. 9.35 L/min
B. 1.29 L/min
C. 0.772 L/min
D. 129 L/min

A. 9.35 L/min
The cardiac output is the volume of blood per minute that is pumped into the systemic circuit. This is determined by the heart rate and the stroke volume. Multiply the heart rate by the stroke volume. 110 * 85 = 9350 mL/min. Divide by 1000 to get units of liters. 9350/1000 = 9.35 L/min.

57.   The type of muscle in the human body that is voluntary is called: (Skill 1.4) (Easy Rigor)

A. Cardiac
B. Sarcomere
C. Smooth
D. Skeletal

D. Skeletal
Of all of the above, only skeletal muscle is under voluntary control. It is found in the skeletal muscles of the human body.

58. **The wrist is an example of what kind of joint. (Skill 1.4)(Moderate Rigor)**

   A. Ball and socket
   B. Pivot
   C. Stationary
   D. Hinge

B. Pivot
The wrist joint is a pivot joint.

59. **The waterproofing protein in the skin is called: (Skill 1.4)(Rigorous)**

   A. keratin
   B. epidermis
   C. collagen
   D. Sebum

A. keratin
The waterproofing protein in the skin is called keratin.

60. **A muscular adaptation to move food through the digestive system is called... (Skill 1.4)(Easy Rigor)**

   A. peristalsis.
   B. passive transport.
   C. voluntary action.
   D. bulk transport.

A. peristalsis
Peristalsis is a process of wave-like contractions. This process allows food to be carried down the pharynx and though the digestive tract.

61. **The role of neurotransmitters in nerve action is... (Skill 1.4)(Easy Rigor)**

   A. to turn off the sodium pump.
   B. to turn off the calcium pump.
   C. to send impulses to neurons.
   D. to send impulses to the body.

A. to turn off the sodium pump
The neurotransmitters turn off the sodium pump, which results in depolarization of the membrane.

62.   Fats are broken down by which substance? (Skill 1.4)(Moderate Rigor)

    A. bile produced in the gall bladder
    B. lipase produced in the gall bladder
    C. glucagons produced in the liver
    D. bile produced in the liver

D. bile produced in the liver
The liver produces bile, which breaks down and emulsifies fatty acids.

63.   Fertilization in humans usually occurs in the... (Skill 1.4)(Easy Rigor)

    A. uterus.
    B. ovary.
    C. fallopian tubes.
    D. vagina.

C. fallopian tubes
Fertilization of the egg by the sperm normally occurs in the fallopian tube. The fertilized egg is then implanted on the uterine lining for development.

64.   All of the following are found in the dermis layer of skin except... (Skill 1.4)(Moderate Rigor)

    A. sweat glands.
    B. keratin.
    C. hair follicles.
    D. blood vessels.

B. keratin
Keratin is a water proofing protein found in the epidermis.

65.   A school-aged boy had the chicken pox as a baby. He will most likely not get this disease again because of... (Skill 1.5)(Moderate Rigor)

    A. passive immunity.
    B. vaccination.
    C. antibiotics.
    D. active immunity.

D. active immunity

Active immunity develops after recovery from an infectious disease, such as the chicken pox, or after vaccination. Passive immunity to some diseases may be passed from one individual to another (from mother to nursing child).

66. **Vaccines are available for all but the following: (Skill 1.5)(Easy Rigor)**

    A. Mumps
    B. Tetanus
    C. Staphylococcus
    D. Measles

C. Staphylococcus
There are vaccines for measles, mumps and tetanus but not for Staphylococcus.

67. **Immune defensive components in the body include all but: (Skill 1.5) (Rigorous)**

    A. humoral immunity
    B. skin barrier
    C. blood brain barrier
    D. cell mediated immunity

C. blood brain barrier
All but blood brain barrier provide protection against pathogens in the body.

68. **Any foreign particle that causes an immune reaction is: (Skill 1.5) (Moderate Rigor)**

    A. an antigen
    B. a histocompatibity complex
    C. an antibody
    D. a vaccine

A. an antigen
An antigen is any foreign particle that results in an immune reaction.

69. **What is responsible for organ transplantation rejection? (Skill 1.5)(Moderate Rigor)**

    A. Antibodies
    B. Major Histocompatibility Complex
    C. Cytotoxic T Cells
    D. Autoimmune factor

B. Major Histocompatibility Complex
The major histocompatibility complex is responsible for organ transplant rejection.

70. **Which of the following is not posttranscriptional processing? (Skill 2.1)(Rigorous)**

    A. 5' capping
    B. intron splicing
    C. polypeptide splicing
    D. 3' polyadenylation

C. polypeptide splicing
The removal of segments of polypeptides is a posttranslational process. The other three are methods of posttranscriptional processing.

71. **The polymerase chain reaction... (Skill 2.1)(Moderate Rigor)**

    A. is a group of polymerases.
    B. is a technique for amplifying DNA.
    C. is a primer for DNA synthesis.
    D. is synthesis of polymerase.

B. is a technique for amplifying DNA
PCR is a technique in which a piece of DNA can be amplified into billions of copies within a few hours.

72. **The area of a DNA nucleotide that varies is the... (Skill 2.1)(Rigorous)**

    A. deoxyribose.
    B. phosphate group.
    C. nitrogenous base.
    D. sugar.

C. nitrogenous base
DNA is made of a 5-carbon sugar (deoxyribose), a phosphate group, and a nitrogenous base. There are four nitrogenous bases in DNA that vary to allow for the four different nucleotides.

73.   A DNA strand has the base sequence of TCAGTA. Its DNA complement would have the following sequence. (Skill 2.1)(Moderate Rigor)

A. ATGACT
B. TCAGTA
C. AGUCAU
D. AGTCAT

D. AGTCAT
The complement strand to a single strand DNA molecule has a complementary sequence to the template strand. T pairs with A and C pairs with G. Therefore, the complement to TCAGTA is AGTCAT.

74.   Genes function in specifying the structure of which molecule? (Skill 2.1)(Rigorous)

A. carbohydrates
B. lipids
C. nucleic acids
D. proteins

D. proteins
Genes contain the sequence of nucleotides that code for amino acids. Amino acids are the building blocks of protein.

75.   What is the correct order of steps in protein synthesis? (Skill 2.1)(Moderate Rigor)

A. transcription, then replication
B. transcription, then translation
C. translation, then transcription
D. replication, then translation

B. transcription, then translation
A DNA strand first undergoes transcription to get a complementary mRNA strand. Translation of the mRNA strand then occurs to result in the tRNA adding the appropriate amino acid for an end product, a protein.

76.   This carries amino acids to the ribosome in protein synthesis. (Skill 2.1) (Easy Rigor)

        A. messenger RNA
        B. ribosomal RNA
        C. transfer RNA
        D. DNA

C. transfer RNA
The tRNA molecule is specific for a particular amino acid. The tRNA has an anticodon sequence that is complementary to the codon. This specifies where the tRNA places the amino acid in protein synthesis.

77.   A protein is sixty amino acids in length. This requires a coded DNA sequence of how many nucleotides? (Skill 2.1)(Rigorous)

        A. 20
        B. 30
        C. 120
        D. 180

D. 180
Each amino acid codon consists of 3 nucleotides. If there are 60 amino acids in a protein, then 60 x 3 = 180 nucleotides.

78.   A DNA molecule has the sequence of ACTATG. What is the anticodon of this molecule? (Skill 2.1)(Moderate Rigor)

        A. UGAUAC
        B. ACUAUG
        C. TGATAC
        D. ACTATG

B. ACUAUG
The DNA is first transcribed into mRNA. Here, the DNA has the sequence ACTATG; therefore, the complementary mRNA sequence is UGAUAC (remember, in RNA, T is U). This mRNA sequence is the codon. The anticodon is the complement to the codon. The anticodon sequence will be ACUAUG (remember, the anticodon is tRNA, so U is present instead of T).

79. **Any change that affects the sequence of bases in a gene is called a(n)... (Skill 2.1)(Rigorous)**

    A. deletion.
    B. polyploid.
    C. mutation.
    D. duplication.

C. mutation
A mutation is an inheritable change in DNA. It may be an error in replication or a spontaneous rearrangement of one ore more segments of DNA. Deletion and duplication are types of mutations. Polyploidy is when an organism has more than two complete chromosome sets.

80. **Segments of DNA can be transferred from the DNA of one organism to another through the use of which of the following? (Skill 2.1)(Moderate Rigor)**

    A. bacterial plasmids
    B. viruses
    C. chromosomes from frogs
    D. plant DNA

A. bacterial plasmids
Plasmids can transfer themselves (and therefore their genetic information) by a process called conjugation. This requires cell-to-cell contact.

81. **The quaternary structure of proteins is: (Skill 2.1)(Rigorous)**

    A. The overall structure of the protein from the aggregation of two or more polypeptide chains.
    B. formed by bonding between the side chains of the amino acids
    C. the coils and folds of polypeptide chains
    D. the protein's unique sequence of amino acids

A. The overall structure of the protein from the aggregation of two or more polypeptide chains
The quaternary structure of proteins is the overall structure of the protein from the aggregation of two or more polypeptide chains.

82. **The enzyme that unwinds DNA during replication is: (Skill 2.1)(Moderate Rigor)**

A. DNAse
B. replicase
C. helicase
D. topoisomerases

C. helicase
The enzyme helicase is involved in unwinding DNA during replication.

83. **A small circular piece of DNA that contains accessory DNA is called:(Skill 2.1)(Moderate Rigor)**

A. mitochondrial DNA
B. messenger RNA
C. transfer DNA
D. plasmid

D. plasmid
A Plasmid is a small, circular piece of accessory DNA.

84. **The order of DNA duplication is the following: (Skill 2.1)(Moderate Rigor)**

A. termination, elongation, initiation
B. initiation, elongation, termination
C. elongation, initiation, termination
D. initiation, termination, elongation

B. initiation, elongation, termination
The order of duplication of DNA is initiation, elongation and termination, followed by posttranscriptional processing.

85. **In DNA, adenine bonds with ____, while cytosine bonds with ____.(Skill 2.1)(Moderate Rigor)**

A. thymine/guanine
B. adenine/cytosine
C. cytosine/adenine
D. guanine/thymine

A. thymine/guanine
In DNA, adenine pairs with thymine and cytosine pairs with guanine because of their nitrogenous base structures.

86. **Which protein structure consists of the coils and folds of polypeptide chains? (Skill 2.1)(Moderate Rigor)**

   A. secondary structure
   B. quaternary structure
   C. tertiary structure
   D. primary structure

A. secondary structure
Primary structure is the protein's unique sequence of amino acids. Secondary structure is the coils and folds of polypeptide chains. The coils and folds are the result of hydrogen bonds along the polypeptide backbone. Tertiary structure is formed by bonding between the side chains of the amino acids. Quaternary structure is the overall structure of the protein from the aggregation of two or more polypeptide chain

87. **Homozygous individuals..... (Skill 2.2)(Easy Rigor)**

   A. have two different alleles.
   B. are of the same species.
   C. have the same features.
   D. have a pair of identical alleles.

D. have a pair of identical alleles
Homozygous individuals have a pair of identical alleles and heterozygous individuals have two different alleles.

88. **The term "phenotype" refers to which of the following? (Skill 2.2)(Moderate Rigor)**

   A. a condition which is heterozygous
   B. the genetic makeup of an individual
   C. a condition which is homozygous
   D. how the genotype is expressed

D. how the genotype is expressed
Phenotype is the physical appearance or expression of an organism due to its genetic makeup (genotype).

89.   **The ratio of brown-eyed to blue-eyed children from the mating of a blue-eyed male to a heterozygous brown-eyed female would be expected to be which of the following? (Skill 2.2)(Moderate Rigor)**

    A. 2:1
    B. 1:1
    C. 1:0
    D. 1:2

B. 1:1

Use a Punnet square to determine the ratio.

	b	b
B	Bb	Bb
b	bb	bb

B = brown eyes, b = blue eyes

Female genotype is on the side and the male genotype is across the top.

The female is heterozygous and her phenotype is brown eyes. This means the dominant allele is for brown eyes. The male expresses the homozygous recessive allele for blue eyes. Their children are expected to have a ratio of brown eyes to blue eyes of 2:2; or 1:1.

90.   **The Law of Segregation defined by Mendel states that... (Skill 2.2)(Moderate Rigor)**

    A. when sex cells form, the two alleles that determine a trait will end up on different gametes.
    B. only one of two alleles is expressed in a heterozygous organism.
    C. the allele expressed is the dominant allele.
    D. alleles of one trait do not affect the inheritance of alleles on another chromosome.

A. when sex cells form, the two alleles that determine a trait will end up on different gametes
The law of segregation states that the two alleles for each trait segregate into different gametes.

91.   **When a white flower is crossed with a red flower, incomplete dominance can be seen by the production of which of the following? (Skill 2.2)(Easy Rigor)**

    A. pink flowers
    B. red flowers
    C. white flowers
    D. red and white flowers

A. pink flowers
Incomplete dominance is when the F_1 generation results in an appearance somewhere between the parents. Red flowers crossed with white flowers results in an F_1 generation with pink flowers.

92.   **A child with type O blood has a father with type A blood and a mother with type B blood. The genotypes of the parents respectively would be which of the following? (Skill 2.2)(Easy Rigor)**

    A. AA and BO
    B. AO and BO
    C. AA and BB
    D. AO and OO

B. AO and BO
Type O blood has 2 recessive O genes. A child receives one allele from each parent; therefore, each parent in this example must have an O allele. The father has type A blood with a genotype of AO and the mother has type B blood with a genotype of BO.

93.   **Crossing over, which increases genetic diversity occurs during which stage(s)? (Skill 2.2)(Rigorous)**

    A. telophase II in meiosis
    B. metaphase in mitosis
    C. interphase in both mitosis and meiosis
    D. prophase I in meiosis

D. prophase I in meiosis
During prophase I of meiosis, the replicated chromosomes condense and pair with their homologues in a process called synapsis. Crossing over, the exchange of genetic material between homologues to further increase diversity, occurs during prophase I of meiosis.

94. **The type of allele dominance found in ABO blood grouping is: (Skill 2.2) (Moderate Rigor)**

    A. Autosomal dominance
    B. Incomplete dominance
    C. Codominance
    D. Complete dominance

C. Cocominance
ABO blood grouping involves codominance.

95. **In a punnet square with a single trait, what are the ratios of genotypes produced? (Skill 2.2)(Moderate Rigor)**

    A. 1:2:2
    B. 2:1:1
    C. 1:1:1
    D. 1:2:1

D. 1:2:1
The punnet square ratio for a single trait is 1:2:1.

96. **The organism's genetic makeup is called: (Skill 2.2)(Moderate Rigor)**

    A. Heterozygote
    B. Genotype
    C. Phenotype
    D. Homozygote

B. Genotype
The genetic makeup is called the genotype.

97. **The law that states that only one of the two possible alleles from each parent is passed on to the offspring is called: (Skill 2.2)(Moderate Rigor)**

    A. The Mendelian Law
    B. The Law of independent assortment
    C. The law of segregation
    D. The allele law

B. The Law of independent assortment
The law of independent assortment states that only one of a pair of alleles is transferred from parent to offspring.

98.   The *lac* operon(Skill 2.3)(Rigorous)

   I.   contains the *lac Z, lac Y,* and *lac A*
        genes
   II. converts glucose to lactose
   III. contains a repressor
   IV. is on when the repressor is
        activated

        A. I
        B. II
        C. III and IV
        D. I and III

D. I and III
The *lac* operon contains the genes that encode for the enzymes used to convert lactose into fuel. It contains three genes: *lac A, lac Z,* and *lac Y.* It also contains a promoter and repressor. When the repressor is activated, the operon is off.

99.   **A genetic engineering advancement in the medical field is... (Skill 2.4)(Easy Rigor)**

        A. gene therapy.
        B. pesticides.
        C. degradation of harmful chemicals.
        D. antibiotics.

A. gene therapy
Gene therapy is the introduction of a normal allele to the somatic cells to replace a defective allele. The medical field has had success in treating patients with a single enzyme deficiency disease. Gene therapy has allowed doctors and scientists to introduce a normal allele that provides the missing enzyme.

100.   **Which of the following is not true regarding restriction enzymes? (Skill 2.4)(Moderate Rigor)**

        A. they aid in transcombination procedures
        B. they are used in genetic engineering
        C. they are named after the bacteria in which they naturally occur
        D. they identify and splice certain base sequences on DNA

A. they aid in transcomination procedures
A restriction enzyme is a bacterial enzyme that cuts foreign DNA at specific locations. The splicing of restriction fragments into a plasmid results in a recombinant plasmid.

101. **What is not one of the modern uses of DNA? (Skill 2.4)(Moderate Rigor)**

    A. PCR technology
    B. Gene therapy
    C. Cloning
    D. Genetic Alignment

D. Genetic Alignment
PCR technology, gene therapy and cloning all come out of working with DNA.

102. **Gel electrophoresis: (Skill 2.4)(Rigorous)**

    A. isolates fragments of DNA for scientific purposes
    B. cannot be used in proteins
    C. requires the polymerase chain reaction
    D. only separates DNA by size

A. isolates fragments of DNA for scientific purposes
Gel electrophoresis separates DNA by size and charge. It can be used in proteins as well and is not dependent on the polymerase chain reaction.

103. **The duplication of genetic material into another cell is called: (Skill 2.4)(Moderate Rigor)**

    A. replicating
    B. cell duplication
    C. cloning
    D. genetic restructuring

C. cloning
Cloning is the duplication of genetic material into another cell.

104. **Electrophoresis separates DNA on the basis of... (Skill 2.4)(Rigorous)**

    A. amount of current.
    B. molecular size.
    C. positive charge of the molecule.
    D. solubility of the gel.

B. molecular size
Electrophoresis uses electrical charges of molecules to separate them according to their size.

105. **Reproductive isolation results in... (Skill 3.1)(Moderate Rigor)**

    A. extinction.
    B. migration.
    C. follilization.
    D. speciation.

D. speciation
Reproductive isolation is caused by any factor that impedes two species from producing viable, fertile hybrids. Reproductive isolation of populations is the primary criterion for recognition of species status.

106. **What is true about natural selection? (Skill 3.1)(Moderate Rigor)**

    A. It acts on an individual genotype
    B. It does not happen currently
    C. It is a phenomenon of animals only
    D. It acts on the individual phenotype

D. It acts on an individual genotype
Natural selection acts on the individual phenotype.

107. **How does diversity aid a population? (Skill 3.1)(Rigorous)**

    A. It provides possible improvements to the population.
    B. Mates are attracted to a diverse population.
    C. Potential mates like conformity.
    D. It increases the DNA differences in the population.

A. It provides possible improvements to the population.
Diversity provides possible improvements to the population.

108. **DNA synthesis results in a strand that is synthesized continuously. This is the... (Skill 3.1)(Rigorous)**

    A. lagging strand.
    B. leading strand.
    C. template strand.
    D. complementary strand.

B. leading strand

As DNA synthesis proceeds along the replication fork, one strand is replicated continuously (the leading strand) and the other strand is replicated discontinuously (the lagging strand).

109. What is not true of diversity? (Skill 3.2)(Moderate Rigor)

    A. Without diversity there would be extinction.
    B. Diversity is increasing all the time.
    C. Fossil evidence supports diversity.
    D. Skeletons are too similar to allow for diversity.

D. Skeletons are too similar to allow for diversity.
The other answers are all true. Without diversity, there would be extinction, diversity is increasing all the time and fossil evidence supports an increase in diversity.

110. Darwin supported the evolutionary Theory of: (Skill 3.2)(Rigorous)

    A. Punctualism
    B. Gradualism
    C. Equilibrium
    D. Convergency

B. Gradualism
Darwin's book is based upon gradualism.

111. What is not true about reproductive isolation? (Skill 3.2)(Moderate Rigor)

    A. It prevents populations from exchanging genes
    B. It can occur by preventing fertilization.
    C. It can result in speciation
    D. It is not a phenomenon of islands.

D. It is not a phenomenon of islands.
Reproductive isolation can result in speciation, can occur by preventing fertilization and prevents populations from exchanging genes. It is a common phenomenon of islands.

112.   **Members of the same species... (Skill 3.2)(Easy Rigor)**

   A. look identical.
   B. never change.
   C. reproduce successfully within their group.
   D. live in the same geographic location.

C. reproduce successfully within their group
Species are defined by the ability to successfully reproduce with members of their own kind.

113.   **Which of the following factors will affect the Hardy-Weinberg law of equilibrium, leading to evolutionary change? (Skill 3.2) (Moderate Rigor)**

   A. no mutations
   B. non-random mating
   C. no immigration or emigration
   D. large population

B.   non-random mating
There are five requirements to keep the Hardy-Weinberg equilibrium stable: no mutation, no selection pressures, an isolated population, a large population, and random mating.

114. **If a population is in Hardy-Weinberg equilibrium and the frequency of the recessive allele is 0.3, what percentage of the population would be expected to be heterozygous? (Skill 3.2)(Rigorous)**

    A. 9%
    B. 49%
    C. 42%
    D. 21%

C. 42%

0.3 is the value of q. Therefore, $q^2 = 0.09$. According to the Hardy-Weinberg equation, $1 = p + q$.

$1 = p + 0.3$.
$p = 0.7$
$p^2 = 0.49$

Next, plug q^2 and p^2 into the equation $1 = p^2 + 2pq + q^2$.

$1 = 0.49 + 2pq + 0.09$ (where $2pq$ is the number of heterozygotes).
$1 = 0.58 + 2pq$
$2pq = 0.42$

Multiply by 100 to get the percent of heterozygotes, 42%.

115. **Which aspect of science does not support evolution? (Skill 3.2)(Moderate Rigor)**

    A. comparative anatomy
    B. organic chemistry
    C. comparison of DNA among organisms
    D. analogous structures

B. organic chemistry
Comparative anatomy is the comparison of characteristics of the anatomies of different species. This includes homologous structures and analogous structures. The comparison of DNA between species is the best known way to place species on the evolution tree. Organic chemistry has nothing to do with evolution.

116.   Evolution occurs in... (Skill 3.2)(Easy Rigor)

   A. individuals.
   B. populations.
   C. organ systems.
   D. cells.

B. populations
Evolution is a change in genotype over time. Gene frequencies shift and change from generation to generation. Populations evolve, not individuals.

117.   Which process contributes most to the large variety of living things in the world today? (Skill 3.2)(Moderate Rigor)

   A. meiosis
   B. asexual reproduction
   C. mitosis
   D. alternation of generations

A. meiosis
During meiosis prophase I crossing over occurs. This exchange of genetic material between homologues increases diversity.

118.   All of the following gases made up the primitive atmosphere except...(Skill 3.4)(Moderate Rigor)

   A. ammonia.
   B. methane.
   C. oxygen.
   D. hydrogen.

C. oxygen
The primitive atmosphere contained ammonia, methane and hydrogen but very little oxygen.

119. **The Endosymbiotic Theory states that... (Skill 3.4)(Rigorous)**

   A. eukaryotes arose from prokaryotes.
   B. animals evolved in close relationships with one another.
   C. prokaryotes arose from eukaryotes.
   D. life arose from inorganic compounds.

A. eukaryotes arose from prokaryotes
The Endosymbiotic theory of the origin of eukaryotes states that eukaryotes arose from symbiotic groups of prokaryotic cells. According to this theory, smaller prokaryotes lived within larger prokaryotic cells, eventually evolving into chloroplasts and mitochondria.

120. **The wing of a bird, human arm, and whale flipper have the same bone structure. These are called... (Skill 3.3)(Moderate Rigor)**

   A. polymorphic structures.
   B. homologous structures.
   C. vestigial structures.
   D. analogous structures.

B. homologous structures
Homologous structures have the same genetic basis (leading to similar appearances), but are used for different functions.

121. **Which of the following is not an abiotic factor? (Skill 3.4)(Moderate Rigor)**

   A. temperature
   B. rainfall
   C. soil quality
   D. bacteria

D. bacteria
Abiotic factors are non-living aspects of an ecosystem. Temperature, rainfall, and soil quality are all abiotic factors. Bacteria is an example of a biotic factor—a living thing.

122. **Which was not a stage in the origin of life? (Skill 3.4)(Moderate Rigor)**

    A. Abiotic
    B. Biotic
    C. Formation of polymers
    D. Accumulation of probionts

B. Biotic
The Abiotic stage was the nonliving stage. Then came the formation of polymers and the accumulation of probionts. The last stage was the origin of heredity.

123. **What is not true about Cladistics? (Skill 3.4)(Rigorous)**

    A. It is the study of phylogenetic relationships of organisms
    B. It involves a branching diagram that uses the development of novel traits to separate groups of organisms.
    C. It distinguishes between the relative importance of the traits.
    D. It shows when traits developed with respect to other traits.

C. It distinguishes between the relative importance of the traits.
Cladistics does not distinguish between the relative importance of the characteristics or traits.

124. **If DDT were present in an ecosystem, which of the following organisms would have the highest concentration in its system? (Skill 4.1)(Rigorous)**

    A. grasshopper
    B. eagle
    C. frog
    D. crabgrass

B. eagle
Chemicals and pesticides accumulate along the food chain. Tertiary consumers have more accumulated toxins than animals at the bottom of the food chain.

125. **What eats secondary consumers? (Skill 4.2)(Moderate Rigor)**

    A. Producers
    B. Tertiary consumers
    C. Primary consumers
    D. Decomposers

B. Tertiary consumers
The tertiary consumers eat the secondary consumers and the secondary consumers eat the primary consumers.

126. **What is true of the water cycle? (Skill 4.2)(Moderate Rigor)**

    A. Two percent of the water is fixed and unavailable.
    B. 75% of available water is groundwater.
    C. The water cycle is driven by the ocean currents.
    D. Surface water is unavailable.

A. Two percent of the water cycle is fixed and is unavailable.
96 percent of available water is groundwater. The water cycle is driven by the sun. Surface water is available.

127. **What is not true of the carbon cycle? (Skill 4.2)(Moderate Rigor)**

    A. Ten percent of all available carbon is in the air.
    B. Carbon dioxide is fixed by glycosylation.
    C. Plants fix carbon in the form of glucose.
    D. Animals release carbon through respiration.

B. Carbon dioxide is fixed by glycosylation.
Ten percent of all available carbon is in the air. Plants fix carbon via photosynthesis to make glucose and animals release carbon through respiration.

128. **Sulfur oxides and nitrogen oxides in the environment react with water to cause... (Skill 4.2)(Moderate Rigor)**

    A. ammonia.
    B. acidic precipitation.
    C. sulfuric acid.
    D. global warming.

B. acidic precipitation
Acidic precipitation is rain, snow, or fog with a pH less than 5.6. It is caused by sulfur oxides and nitrogen oxides that react with water in the air to form acids that fall down to Earth as precipitation.

129.   In the comparison of respiration to photosynthesis, which statement is true? (Skill 4.2)(Rigorous)

A. oxygen is a waste product in photosynthesis but not in respiration
B. glucose is produced in respiration but not in photosynthesis
C. carbon dioxide is formed in photosynthesis but not in respiration
D. water is formed in respiration but not in photosynthesis

A. oxygen is a waste product in photosynthesis but not in respiration
In photosynthesis, water is split and the oxygen is given off as a waste product. In respiration, water and carbon dioxide are the waste products.

130.   Which term is not associated with the water cycle? (Skill 4.2)(Moderate Rigor)

A. precipitation
B. transpiration
C. fixation
D. evaporation

C. fixation
Water is recycled through the processes of evaporation and precipitation. Transpiration is the evaporation of water from leaves. Fixation is not associated with the water cycle.

131.   All of the following are density independent factors that affect a population except... (Skill 4.2)(Easy Rigor)

A. temperature.
B. rainfall.
C. predation.
D. soil nutrients.

C. predation
As a population increases, the competition for resources is intense and the growth rate declines. This is a density-dependent factor. An example of this would be predation. Density-independent factors affect the population regardless of its size. Examples of density-independent factors are rainfall, temperature, and soil nutrients.

132. High humidity and temperature stability are present in which of the following biomes? (Skill 4.2)(Easy Rigor)

    A. taiga
    B. deciduous forest
    C. desert
    D. tropical rain forest

D. tropical rain forest
A tropical rain forest is located near the equator. Its temperature is at a constant 25 degrees C and the humidity is high due to the rainfall that exceeds 200 cm per year.

133. Which trophic level has the highest ecological efficiency? (Skill 4.2)(Moderate Rigor)

    A. decomposers
    B. producers
    C. tertiary consumers
    D. secondary consumers

B. producers
The amount of energy that is transferred between trophic levels is called the ecological efficiency. The visual of this is represented in a pyramid of productivity. The producers have the greatest amount of energy and are at the bottom of this pyramid.

134. Oxygen created in photosynthesis comes from the breakdown of... (Skill 4.2)(Easy Rigor)

    A. carbon dioxide.
    B. water.
    C. glucose.
    D. carbon monoxide.

B. water
In photosynthesis, water is split; the hydrogen atoms are pulled to carbon dioxide which is taken in by the plant and ultimately reduced to make glucose. The oxygen from the water is given off as a waste product.

135. **What is not true of decomposers? (Skill 4.2)(Rigorous)**

    A. Decomposers recycle the carbon accumulated in durable organic material
    B. Ammonification is the decomposition of organic nitrogen back to ammonia.
    C. Decomposers add phosphorous back to the soil
    D. Decomposers belong to the Genus Escherichia.

D. Decomposers belong to the Genus Escherichia.
Decomposers recycle phosphorus and carbon and undergo ammonification.

136. **A virus that can remain dormant until a certain environmental condition causes its rapid increase is said to be... (Skill 4.3)(Moderate Rigor)**

    A. lytic.
    B. benign.
    C. saprophytic.
    D. lysogenic.

D. lysogenic
Lysogenic viruses remain dormant until something initiates it to break out of the host cell.

137. **A clownfish is protected by the sea anemone's tentacles. In turn, the anemone receives uneaten food from the clownfish. This is an example of... (Skill 4.3)(Easy Rigor)**

    A. mutualism.
    B. parasitism.
    C. commensalisms.
    D. competition.

A. mutualism
Neither the clownfish nor the anemone cause harmful effects towards one another and they both benefit from their relationship. Mutualism is when two species that occupy a similar space benefit from their relationship.

138. **Which of the following does not result in the detriment of one species and the advancement of another? (Skill 4.3)(Moderate Rigor)**

    A. Parasitism
    B. Mutualism
    C. Predation
    D. Herbivory

B. Mutualism
Parasitism, Herbivory and Predation all result in the detriment of one species.

139. **In an experiment measuring the growth of bacteria at different temperatures, identify the independent variable. (Skill 5.2)(Moderate Rigor)**

    A. growth of number of colonies
    B. temperature
    C. type of bacteria used
    D. light intensity

B. temperature
The independent variable is controlled by the experimenter. Here, the temperature is controlled to determine its effect on the growth of bacteria (dependent variable).

140. **Primary succession occurs after... (Skill 5.3)(Moderate Rigor)**

    A. nutrient enrichment.
    B. a forest fire.
    C. bare rock is exposed after a water table recedes.
    D. a housing development is built.

C. bare rock is exposed after a water table recedes
Primary succession occurs where life never existed before, such as flooded areas or a new volcanic island. It is only after the water recedes that the rock is able to support new life.

141. **A scientific theory... ...(Skill 6.1)(Moderate Rigor)**

    A. proves scientific accuracy.
    B. is never rejected.
    C. results in a medical breakthrough.
    D. may be altered at a later time.

D. may be altered at a later time
Scientific theory is usually accepted and verified information but can always be changed at anytime. Many theories have had to be altered after advances in technology gave scientists a clearer view.

142. **Which is the correct order of methodology? 1) testing a revised explanation, 2) setting up a controlled experiment to test an explanation, 3) drawing a conclusion, 4) suggesting an explanation for observations, and 5) comparing observed results to hypothesized results (Skill 6.1)(Rigorous)**

    A. 4, 2, 3, 1, 5
    B. 3, 1, 4, 2, 5
    C. 4, 2, 5, 1, 3
    D. 2, 5, 4, 1, 3

C. 4, 2, 5, 1, 3
The first step in scientific inquiry is posing a question to be answered. Next, a hypothesis is formed to provide a plausible explanation. An experiment is then proposed and performed to test this hypothesis. A comparison between the predicted and observed results is the next step. Conclusions are then formed and it is determined whether the hypothesis is correct or incorrect. If incorrect, the next step is to form a new hypothesis and repeat the process.

143. **Given a choice, which is the most desirable method of heating a substance in the lab? (Skill 7.4) (Easy Rigor)**

    A. alcohol burner
    B. gas burner
    C. bunsen burner
    D. hot plate

D. hot plate
A hotplate is the only heat source from the choices above that does not have an open flame. The use of a hot plate will reduce the risk of fire and injury to students.

144. Biological waste should be disposed of... (Skill 7.4)(Easy Rigor)

  A. in the trash can.
  B. under a fume hood.
  C. in the broken glass box.
  D. in an autoclavable biohazard bag.

D. in an autoclavable biohazard bag
Biological material should never be stored near food or water used for human consumption. All biological material should be appropriately labeled. All blood and body fluids should be put in a well-contained container with a secure lid to prevent leaking. All biological waste should be disposed of in biological hazardous waste bags.

145. Chemicals should be stored... (Skill 7.4)(Easy Rigor)

  A. in a cool dark room.
  B. in a dark room.
  C. according to their reactivity with other substances.
  D. in a double locked room.

C. according to their reactivity with other substances
All chemicals should be stored with other chemicals of similar reactivity. Failure to do so could result in an undesirable chemical reaction.

146. Who should be notified in the case of a serious chemical spill? (Skill 7.4)(Moderate Rigor)

  I. the custodian
  II. the fire department
  III. the chemistry teacher
  IV. the administration

  A. I
  B. II
  C. II and III
  D. II and IV

D. II and IV
For large spills, the school administration and the local fire department should be notified.

147. **The "Right to Know" law states... (Skill 7.4)(Rigorous)**

   A. the inventory of toxic chemicals checked against the "Substance List" be available.
   B. that students are to be informed of alternatives to dissection.
   C. that science teachers are to be informed of student allergies.
   D. that students are to be informed of infectious microorganisms used in lab.

A. the inventory of toxic chemicals checked against the "Substance List" be available
The right to know law pertains to chemical substances in the lab. Employees should check the material safety data sheets and the substance list for potential hazards in the lab.

148. **In which situation would a science teacher be liable? (Skill 7.4)(Moderate Rigor)**

   A. a teacher leaves to receive an emergency phone call and a student slips and falls
   B. a student removes their goggles and gets dissection fluid in their eye
   C. a faulty gas line results in a fire
   D. a student cuts himself with a scalpel

A. a teacher leaves to receive an emergency phone call and a student slips and falls
A teacher has an obligation to be present in the lab at all times. If the teacher needs to leave, an appropriate substitute is needed.

149. **Which statement best defines negligence? (Skill 7.4)(Easy Rigor)**

   A. failure to give oral instructions for those with reading disabilities
   B. failure to exercise ordinary care
   C. inability to supervise a large group of students
   D. reasonable anticipation that an event may occur

B. failure to exercise ordinary care
Negligence is the failure to exercise ordinary or reasonable care.

150. **Which item should always be used when using chemicals with noxious vapors? (Skill 7.4)(Easy Rigor)**

    A. eye protection
    B. face shield
    C. fume hood
    D. lab apron

C. fume hood

Fume hoods are designed to protect the experimenter from chemical fumes. The three other choices do not prevent chemical fumes from entering the respiratory system.

XAMonline, INC. 21 Orient Ave. Melrose, MA 02176

Toll Free number 800-509-4128

TO ORDER Fax 781-662-9268 OR www.XAMonline.com

CALIFORNIA SUBJECT EXAMINATIONS - CSET - 2008

PO#   Store/School:

Address 1:

Address 2 (Ship to other):

City, State Zip

Credit card number_____-_____-_____-_____   expiration_____

EMAIL _____

PHONE   **FAX**

ISBN	TITLE	Qty	Retail	Total
978-1-58197-595-6	RICA Reading Instruction Competence Assessment		$24.95	
978-1-58197-596-3	CBEST CA Basic Educational Skills		$19.95	
978-1-58197-901-5	CSET French Sample Test 149, 150		$15.00	
978-1-58197-622-9	CSET Spanish 145, 146, 147		$59.95	
978-1-58197-803-2	CSET MSAT Multiple Subject 101, 102, 103		$28.95	
978-1-58197-261-0	CSET English 105, 106, 107		$59.95	
978-1-58197-608-3	CSET Foundational-Level Mathematics 110, 111		$59.95	
978-1-58197-285-6	CSET Mathematics 110, 111, 112		$32.95	
978-1-58197-340-2	CSET Social Science 114, 115		$59.95	
978-1-58197-342-6	CSET General Science 118, 119		$59.95	
978-1-58197-585-7	CSET Biology-Life Science 120, 124		$59.95	
978-1-58197-395-2	CSET Chemistry 121, 125		$59.95	
978-1-58197-571-0	CSET Earth and Planetary Science 122, 126		$59.95	
978-1-58197-817-9	CSET Physics 123, 127		$59.95	
978-1-58197-299-3	CSET Physical Education, 129, 130, 131		$59.95	
978-1-58197-813-1	CSET Art Sample Subtest 140		$15.00	
			SUBTOTAL	
			Ship	$8.70
			TOTAL	